The Mood
Elevator

The Mood Elevator

Take Charge of Your Feelings,
Become a Better You

Larry Senn

BK

Berrett–Koehler Publishers, Inc.
a BK Life book

Berrett-Koehler Publishers, Inc.
1333 Broadway, Suite 1000, Oakland, CA 94612-1921
Tel: (510) 817-2277   Fax: (510) 817-2278   www.bkconnection.com

Ordering Information

Quantity sales. Special discounts are available on quantity purchases by
corporations, associations, and others. For details, contact the "Special Sales
Department" at the Berrett-Koehler address above.

Individual sales. Berrett-Koehler publications are available through most
bookstores. They can also be ordered directly from Berrett-Koehler:

Tel: (800) 929-2929; Fax: (802) 864-7626; www.bkconnection.com.

Orders for college textbook/course adoption use. Please contact
Berrett-Koehler:

Tel: (800) 929-2929; Fax: (802) 864-7626.

Orders by U.S. trade bookstores and wholesalers. Please contact Ingram
Publisher Services, Tel: (800) 509-4887; Fax: (800) 838-1149; E-mail:
customer.service@ingrampublisherservices.com; or visit www.ingram
publisherservices.com/Ordering for details about electronic ordering.

Berrett-Koehler and the BK logo are registered trademarks of
Berrett-Koehler Publishers, Inc.

Printed in the United States of America

Berrett-Koehler books are printed on long-lasting acid-free paper. When
it is available, we choose paper that has been manufactured by environ-
mentally responsible processes. These may include using trees grown in
sustainable forests, incorporating recycled paper, minimizing chlorine in
bleaching, or recycling the energy produced at the paper mill.

Library of Congress Cataloging-in-Publication Data
Names: Senn, Larry E., author.
Title: The mood elevator : take charge of your feelings, become a better you
/ Larry Senn.
Description: First Edition. | Oakland, CA : Berrett-Koehler Publishers,
[2017] | Includes bibliographical references and index.
Identifiers: LCCN 2017012331 | ISBN 9781523084616 (pbk.)
Subjects: LCSH: Mind and body. | Thought and thinking. | Interpersonal
relations. | Self-actualization (Psychology)
Classification: LCC BF161 .S375 2017 | DDC 152.4—dc23
LC record available at https://lccn.loc.gov/2017012331

21   20   19   18   17   10   9   8   7   6   5   4   3   2   1

Cover design by Kirk DouPonce, DogEared Design. Interior design and
composition by Gary Palmatier, Ideas to Images. Elizabeth von Radics,
copyeditor; Mike Mollett, proofreader; Rachel Rice, indexer.

To my wife and soulmate, Bernadette, and to our five children Kevin, Darin, Jason, Kendra, and Logan.

You keep me young at heart and provide the love and the life lessons that help me gracefully ride the Mood Elevator in life.

Contents

Preface   ix

CHAPTER **1**
The Mood Elevator   1

CHAPTER **2**
What Drives the Mood Elevator?   13

CHAPTER **3**
Up the Mood Elevator: The Big Payoffs   23

CHAPTER **4**
Escaping Unhealthy Normal   41

CHAPTER **5**
Braking Your Mood Elevator:
The Power of Curiosity   57

CHAPTER **6**
Interrupting Your Pattern   67

CHAPTER **7**
Feeding the Thoughts You Favor   77

CHAPTER **8**
Living in Mild Preference   89

CHAPTER **9**

Shifting Your Set Point:
The Wellness Equation 99

CHAPTER **10**

Quieting Your Mind 115

CHAPTER **11**

Cultivating Gratitude 121

CHAPTER **12**

Honoring Our Separate Realities 137

CHAPTER **13**

Nurturing Faith and Optimism 155

CHAPTER **14**

Dealing With Your Down Days 165

CHAPTER **15**

Relationships and the Mood Elevator 171

CHAPTER **16**

Pointers for Riding the Mood Elevator 175

How This Book Came to Be 179

Notes 187

Bibliography 191

Acknowledgments 193

Index 195

About the Author 211

Preface

I invite you to join me on a journey of understanding about a concept that can be life-altering: the Mood Elevator.

I had been researching and gathering ideas for this book for several years but had allowed a busy personal and professional life to keep me from completing it. Then one day we conducted an off-site meeting on personal purpose for all employees at my company, Senn Delaney, a Heidrick & Struggles company. After taking the time to reflect on how I hoped to make a difference in the world, I concluded that my purpose was to "provide understanding and inspiration to an ever-widening circle of people, beginning with my family, to live life at their best mentally, emotionally, physically, and spiritually."

As soon as I articulated that, I knew I needed to complete my book. I saw sharing these ideas with the world as one of the best ways to bring that purpose to life.

I founded Senn Delaney almost four decades ago to fulfill a vision of enhancing the spirit and performance of organizations by systematically shaping their cultures. Today it is widely recognized as the most successful culture-shaping consulting firm in the world. The Mood Elevator is just one of many concepts Senn Delaney uses as part of its overall process to create thriving organizational cultures.

The Mood Elevator has been enthusiastically embraced by hundreds of thousands of employees of Senn Delaney clients around the world. Many of them have expressed a desire to learn more about the Mood Elevator and to share it with friends and loved ones. The book is designed for them, as well as for others who may learn about the Mood Elevator for the first time through this book.

While many ideas in the book are taught to clients in Senn Delaney sessions, a number of the ideas and suggestions, including those about wellness, fitness, and healthy living, come as a result of my own personal life journey and do not necessarily reflect the views of Senn Delaney or its work with organizations.

My focus in writing *The Mood Elevator* is simply to benefit individuals by bringing them ideas I have discovered through my life experiences. My hope is that the book will help you take charge of your emotions and be a better you.

Larry E. Senn

The Mood
Elevator

The Mood Elevator

*I know of no more encouraging fact than the
unquestionable ability of man to elevate his life
by a conscious endeavor.... To affect the quality of
the day, that is the highest of arts.*

—HENRY DAVID THOREAU

Let me tell you a story about my friend John. I wonder
whether you've ever known someone like him.

In many ways John is a lucky guy. He has a wonderful
wife, two smart young kids, and an interesting job in the
marketing division of a company we'll call Tip-Top Products. In the eyes of many people, John is on top of the world.
But as our story begins, John is feeling very upset. He has
just left his office at Tip-Top Products at closing time and is
on his way home as usual, but he decides to stop for a few
minutes at a nearby park to try to regain his composure.

John is troubled because of a conversation he had just
a few minutes earlier with a colleague named Fran.

"Say, John," Fran remarked, poking her head into his office. "Have you heard the latest rumor about next year's budget? It's all over the company."

"Haven't heard a thing," John replied. "What's the scoop?"

"Well, it's just a rumor, of course, but the word is that the board is worried about this quarter's profit downturn. They're supposedly talking about downsizing. And from what I hear, your division might be on the chopping block."

John felt a knot beginning to form in his stomach. "Really? Who told you that?"

Fran shook her head. "I'm not supposed to say," she replied. "And it may turn out to be nothing, but I thought you'd want to know."

"Thanks, Fran," John answered. Suddenly his plans for the evening—enjoying dinner with the family followed by a football game on TV—seemed utterly inconsequential. Fears and worries flooded his mind as he left the office.

Now, sitting on a park bench a few minutes later, John thinks about the possibility of being laid off and the dire consequences that could have. What if he can't find another job? Will his kids be able to go to college? Will he lose his home? (A neighbor got laid off a year earlier and had to move back in with his parents—it can happen that easily.) Can his ego handle being fired? How will he break the news to his wife? Susie is such a worrier—and maybe she'll figure he must have done something wrong to deserve being let go. *She'll probably wish she'd married her old boyfriend Ben after all—isn't he a hotshot lawyer by now? And who could blame her? She deserves better than to be hitched to a failure like me.* John finds his mood rapidly plunging from anxious, to worried, to downright depressed.

Then his thoughts turn back to Tip-Top Products. He recalls all the years of hard work he's put in and the contributions he's made to the company's success. How had the bosses gotten the company into this position? And how did they decide that downsizing would be the solution? Was the decision made just to benefit the people at the top? *I bet those fat cats in the executive suite aren't facing any pay cuts—let alone layoffs,* John fumes. His feeling of depression gives way to a sense of resentment and self-righteous anger.

Suddenly he remembers Fran's words: "It may turn out to be nothing." That's true, isn't it? Rumors like this have circulated before and turned out to be just hot air. And Fran is always one of the first to spread the latest scuttlebutt—true or not. John's anxiety begins to lift. Heaving a sigh of relief, he says to himself, *It's probably not true at all! After all, one quarter of bad financial results is no big deal. I bet our profits are going to be back to normal in no time—and the board probably thinks so, too.* He gets up from the park bench and heads toward home.

Strolling through the park, John finds his thoughts going in a different direction. He says to himself, *Maybe this rumor is really a wakeup call for me. I've been trying to work up the courage to leave Tip-Top for the past year and look for something better—like a job at that high-tech startup my buddy Ron just joined. Maybe now is the time to do it.* He begins imagining the exciting changes that a new career path could bring—a higher salary, a bigger office, maybe a company car and a country club membership. Picturing the admiring expression on Susie's face when he brings home a handsome bonus check from his new employers, he becomes quite excited, even inspired. He vows to get to work on updating his résumé as soon as possible—maybe tonight!

John's buoyant mood is mellowed by the sight of two kids, about the same age as his own, climbing on a jungle gym. *After all,* he thinks, *isn't that what really matters— having a family you love?* There's a spring in John's step as he exits the park and heads for home, looking forward to some quality time with his wife and kids. As for the rumor about Tip-Top, that can wait till morning, when he will compare notes with his closest colleagues and figure out what's *really* going on.

∾

You may have never had to deal with a downsizing rumor like the one that sent John into a tizzy that afternoon, but I'll bet you've experienced emotional ups and downs like he went through. It's a common, almost universal experience—especially in a world as full of unpredictable, uncontrollable changes and chances as ours. As you can tell from the story, John's emotional ups and downs simply followed his thinking. It's our thinking that takes us on this kind of wild ride in life.

I call this "riding the Mood Elevator"—but you might call it simply the human condition. It's our moment-to-moment experience of life. The Mood Elevator carries us up and down as we swing through a wide range of emotions. Those feelings play a major role in defining the quality of our lives, as well as our effectiveness in dealing with daily challenges.

We all ride up and down the Mood Elevator every day. So wouldn't it be great if we knew the right buttons to push to stay among the top floors? And wouldn't it be helpful if we knew how to make our visits to the lower floors less unpleasant and shorter in duration? Providing the keys that can help you control your rides on the Mood Elevator is the main purpose of this book.

Let's begin by looking at the Mood Elevator and the various floors it visits. The Mood Elevator map is based on my own experience, as well as input from hundreds of groups and tens of thousands of people who attended seminars designed or conducted by Senn Delaney and our client facilitators. In reality, we each have our own unique set of Mood Elevator floors, but most of the levels shown on the map are probably familiar to you—and it's likely you've visited them at one point or another in your life.

Think about your own travels on the Mood Elevator, beginning with your visits to the upper floors. These are

moments, hours, or days when we are lighthearted. We
are in touch with things we are grateful for in our lives; we
feel secure, confident, creative, and resourceful. We are not
easily bothered by people and situations and are less apt to
"sweat the small stuff." We are more curious than judgmental and are inclined to see the humor in things. We tackle
life's challenges with a sense of ease and grace, feel connected to the flow of life, and may even find ourselves able
to tap into a source of universal wisdom or intelligence. At
times like these, we are operating "up the Mood Elevator,"
and they are times we are likely to remember with a feeling
of satisfaction and pleasure.

But being human means that we spend some time
"down the Mood Elevator," as well. These are times when our
lives don't look or feel as good, times when we feel insecure
and worried. We find we are easily irritated and bothered by
people or circumstances; we may feel judgmental, defensive,
and self-righteous. Or we may feel vaguely "down," troubled,
or depressed. When we are down the Mood Elevator, our
emotions may range from quite passive (listless, lethargic, or
blue) to very intense and active (resentful, fearful, or angry).

We'll use the Mood Elevator as our map of human
experience throughout this book. It is simple and straight-
forward, and it fits well with my subjective perceptions of
how my moods tend to shift. I am not claiming that the
Mood Elevator has been scientifically validated; it is simply
a tool that I have found very effective in my own life—and
many others with whom I have shared it agree.

The Mood Elevator

Grateful

Wise/insightful

Creative/innovative

Resourceful

Hopeful/optimistic

Appreciative

Patient/understanding

Sense of humor

Flexible/adaptive

Curious/interested

Impatient/frustrated

Irritated/bothered

Worried/anxious

Defensive/insecure

Judgmental/blaming

Self-righteous

Stressed/burned-out

Angry/hostile

Depressed

To begin reflecting on the Mood Elevator and its role in your life, ask yourself the following questions:

▶ Which floors are most familiar to me as part of my normal day-to-day experience of life?

▶ Which floors most commonly define my temperament? On which floors would the people who know me best most often expect to find me?

▶ Which floors would I like to visit more often in my life? On which floors would I like to spend less time?

▶ Which floors do I most often get stuck on when I am having a bad day?

▶ Which floors do I tend to land on when my mood begins to drop?

▶ Which floors do I visit on days when I am feeling most productive, creative, and happy?

Everyone experiences the Mood Elevator in their unique way. For me, the feeling of gratitude tends to mark those moments when I'm on the very highest floor of my personal elevator. When I slow down, quiet my mind, and set aside the preoccupations and pressures of the day, I become aware of the gratitude I feel toward my wife, Bernadette, and our five children. The same sense of gratitude wells up in me when my teenage son, Logan, or one of my other kids gives me a hug and says, "I love you, Dad," or when I pause to experience a beautiful sunset that paints the sky with a multitude of amazing colors.

Good things seem to happen to me when I am on the upper floors of my Mood Elevator. I find myself feeling creative and resourceful. Ideas and answers come more easily, and solutions to problems seem more accessible. The feelings of love, hope, patience, and curiosity that I experience make my life richer and enable me to contribute more to my family and friends, to my church, and to my chosen life's work.

In fact, the pleasure I take from my days on the upper floors is what drove me to write this book—and also what enabled me to turn that desire into a reality. When I am on one of the lower floors, creative thoughts don't come at all. Frozen by writer's block, I find it hard to think of examples or stories to illustrate my ideas—and the ones I do manage to come up with appear silly and worthless. By contrast, there are days when metaphors and images come pouring out, as if I am connected to a source of inspiration and ideas greater than myself—some fount of universal intelligence and original thought that I only have to tap into.

One of the warning signs I've learned to recognize that tells me I'm heading down the Mood Elevator is when I notice myself becoming more impatient, more easily irritated or bothered. A minor inconvenience, mistake, or misunderstanding that I would ordinarily shrug off or laugh about seems to get under my skin, provoking annoyance or anger when I'm sinking toward those lower floors.

I am sure you can recall experiences from your travels on the Mood Elevator in your own life. Most people have a natural desire to experience life on the higher floors more often and more consistently. Who wouldn't want to worry less, feel less stress, and be irritated and bothered less often? Who wouldn't want to feel more gratitude, love, humor, and lightness? Who wouldn't want to experience a heightened degree of creativity, curiosity, flexibility, and resilience?

What's more, the benefits of life on the upper floors are long lasting and cumulative. The more time we spend at those higher levels, the better our lives tend to go—because the upper floors on the Mood Elevator are where we function at our best, thinking most clearly, making the smartest choices, and behaving most creatively. Think about it: Which floors would you rather be on when you are trying to build—or repair—an important personal relationship? When discussing a sensitive issue with someone you love? When tackling a complex problem at work? When making an important life decision?

For most of us, the answer is obvious. The higher levels on the Mood Elevator lead to more success with less stress— to healthier relationships, greater personal productivity, and a better quality of life. No matter how you personally define success—regardless of what realms of achievement and happiness are most important to you—the upper floors on the Mood Elevator are a better place from which to parent, to lead, and to build a career.

Just imagine how different your life, work, and relationships might be if you spent a lot more time on the upper floors—and if you knew how to minimize the negative impact on yourself and others from your inevitable visits to the lower floors.

When I talk with people about the Mood Elevator, almost everyone immediately recognizes the concept—yet very few have ever thought about their life experience in this way. That's probably because they assume that the Mood Elevator is "just the way life is," a basic truth of human existence that we can't change and that it's therefore pointless to think about.

It is true that being human means we all spend time riding up and down the Mood Elevator. We all will visit most of the floors at one time or another. But the time we spend at the various levels differs dramatically. Have you ever known someone who seemed to have permanently moved in to the floors labeled *impatient/frustrated, worried/anxious,* and *judgmental/blaming*? On the other hand, have you ever been lucky enough to know someone who was habitually in residence on the floors named *resourceful, hopeful/optimistic,* and *patient/understanding*? The choices we make can have a significant impact on which floors we spend the majority of our time on—and that, in turn, has a huge effect on the people we come in contact with and the quality of our lives.

There's much more to say about the Mood Elevator. The relationships among the different floors can be complex, and moving from one floor to another can sometimes be quite challenging. In the chapters to come, we delve more deeply into the realities of navigating life on the Mood Elevator.

For now, the key takeaway is this: The central purpose of this book is to provide you with some techniques you can use to increase the amount of time you spend up the Mood Elevator and reduce the duration and negative impacts of operating on the lower floors. The principles I share in the chapters that follow have already enabled countless people to spend more time on the upper floors, and I believe they can do the same for you.

What Drives the Mood Elevator?

Man is made or unmade by himself...and [as] the lord of his own thoughts, man holds the key to every situation.

—JAMES ALLEN

Becoming skilled at riding the Mood Elevator requires an understanding of what controls the vehicle.

So, what drives the Mood Elevator? Where do the moods that carry us higher and lower come from? The answer may surprise you because it is not obvious, nor is it what most people think, and simply understanding the answer can have an enormous impact on your life.

Some moods appear to come upon us out of the blue, like an unpredictable change in the weather. We get out of bed and find we have a bit of an attitude—one that makes us feel grouchy and irritable for no reason at all. Moods like this are the source of the old saying *I got up on the wrong side of the bed.*

But many moods seem to have a more concrete source. One obvious factor is the events in our daily lives. It often appears on the surface that the moods we experience derive from things that happen to us or things that people say to us. Think about my friend John, whose story I told in chapter 1. If asked, John would probably say that his whirlwind of moods was caused by his conversation with Fran, who passed along the rumor about possible layoffs at Tip-Top Products. Most people believe that their moods are caused by external circumstances—and this applies particularly to negative moods, which carry us to the lower floors. Something occurs that we don't like, or someone does something that "pushes our buttons."

You can think of any number of examples: A loved one makes a negative comment about your clothes or your cooking, or they fail to thank you when you really went out of your way to do something nice for them. The stock market goes down again, putting a hurt on your retirement investments. You step on the bathroom scale and don't like the number you see. Your teenager brings home a date with a few too many piercings for your taste. You accidentally run a red light and get stuck with a costly ticket. Your boss or a colleague blames you unfairly for something you didn't do—or, worse, blames you *fairly* for something you *did* do! I think you get the picture.

We all encounter challenges like these on a daily—if not hourly—basis, but they don't really explain where our moods come from. After all, a moment's reflection will tell you that some moods have no apparent connection to outside events. We feel good or bad "for no real reason," and in fact these moods often end up affecting our behavior and experiences rather than the other way around. In other cases, events that might ordinarily trigger a change in our mood simply don't do so.

Yes, sometimes a critical remark from your spouse can cause your mood to plummet, provoking defensiveness or anger—but on some days you shrug it off or even offer a playful, teasing response that evokes laughter on both sides. Sometimes a stock market plunge may produce anxiety or depression—but other times it compels you to call your financial adviser and schedule a long-overdue conversation about how best to rebalance your investment portfolio. Sometimes a reprimand from the boss triggers hostility and resentment—but other times you use it as an opportunity to figure out how you can improve your work methods so that you won't make the same mistake again.

We're not automatons, reacting mechanically and predictably to outside stimuli. We're human beings, and the ways we respond to circumstances vary—depending not on outside events but rather on what happens inside our heads. *There may be events that stimulate our thoughts, but it is the thoughts that determine our moods.*

Think back to my friend John. Yes, Fran's comment launched the cascade of feelings that sent him on his wild ride down (and then up) the Mood Elevator. But each shift in the elevator's direction was driven by a thought inside John's head, from his memories of the hard work he'd devoted to Tip-Top Products to his fantasies about a possible future as a rising executive at his buddy Ron's high-tech firm. John's story illustrates the fact that it's not the circumstances of our life that create our moods—it's what we make of those circumstances. The controlling variable between the event and the mood that results is *what we make of it*—our thoughts.[1]

We see this truth in everyday life. You may end a difficult day feeling tired, a bit overwhelmed by thoughts of what you have to face tomorrow, and a bit discouraged by reflections on the things you didn't accomplish today. Then you get a good night's sleep, rise in the sunshine and take a walk or run, and find that, almost miraculously, life is fine. You head off to a new day at work feeling hopeful, ready to tackle that list of challenges.

Nothing in your life circumstances has changed. The only thing that's changed is your thinking about it.

The same applies to our most intimate relationships. I have five children who range in age from 16 to 52. With my three older boys, who are now in their forties and fifties, I went through all the phases, from changing diapers and sleepless nights; to teaching them to swim, body-board, water-ski, and ride dirt bikes; to college graduations. I remarried more than 36 years ago, and after a number of years Bernadette said she wanted to start a brand-new family. We had Kendra when I was 55 and Logan when I was 65. The age difference between them makes Logan almost like an only child, so I often end up being his playmate—from paddleboarding to water-skiing to zip-lining. And I watch many dawn-to-dusk club volleyball tournaments, since that's his chosen sport.

This unusual set of experiences stimulates a wide range of thoughts that could put me on very different levels on the Mood Elevator. On most weekend or vacation mornings when Logan says, "Let's go, Dad!" I reflect on all the positive things Logan has brought into my life. Because he sees the world through the fresh and curious eyes of a child, he helps me learn and grow. And being his playmate has increased my commitment to health and fitness so that I can keep up with him. I usually respond to Logan's invitation by yelling, "Last one in the water is a rotten egg!" and leading him on a merry chase.

But once in a while, my thoughts travel in the opposite direction. On an occasional weekend or vacation when I'd rather sleep in to relax or recharge, the thought of mustering the energy to go to Wet 'n Wild water park or to jump off the rocks at Waimea Bay provokes thoughts like *What was I thinking—adding another kid to the family so late in life?! I could be catching a few more winks or enjoying my favorite book in the hammock instead of wearing myself out.* I groan, turn over in bed, and pull the covers over my head (usually in vain, of course).

What has changed? It's the same Logan and the same life I chose. It's what I make of it—my thinking—that makes the difference. Yes, life is what we make of it.

The Movie in Your Mind

A while back Senn Delaney hired a new consultant named Deborah, who had previously worked for a company in Houston. Because our consultants fly to most engagements, they can live wherever they choose, and Deb elected to stay in Houston.

Shortly after Deb joined us and began her training, I scheduled a sales call with the CEO of a major utility company in Houston. I decided to invite Deb to join me. I thought that participating in the meeting would give her a chance to hear how we presented ourselves to a prospective client, and it might yield some work for her in her hometown.

It was an innocent, well-intentioned invitation. I had no idea how it would affect Deb's thinking.

Much later Deb recounted to me the thoughts that had cascaded through her mind:

> *A sales call with the chairman of my new company!?*
> *But I'm so new. I'm just getting to know Senn Delaney.*
> *What if I perform badly? I'm not a salesperson; I'm a*
> *consultant. What if I say something stupid? What if*
> *I embarrass my boss and we lose the sale? I could get*
> *fired! That would look awful on my résumé. I took a*
> *risk leaving my longtime employer, and I can't go back*
> *now. What if I can't get another job? My oldest child*
> *won't be able to start college. I could lose my house.*

Before she got her imagination under control, Deb had pictured herself homeless, living in a cardboard box under the freeway.

In fact, the meeting unfolded quite differently than Deb had feared. The three of us got along wonderfully—in fact, it turned out that Deb attended the same church as the utility company CEO, and they had mutual friends. Senn Delaney won the consulting engagement, and Deb had an assignment in her hometown to launch her new career. It was later that Deb shared with me the fearful thoughts she'd subjected herself to, and we both had a good laugh over it.

But Deb is far from unique. We all go through life interpreting everything that happens (or doesn't happen) and projecting a story about what it means. It's as though we are making a movie in our heads. We take whatever our thinking is and make it feel as real as our emotions and physical reactions can—just the way a Hollywood special effects department can turn a fantasy into a virtual reality. And thanks to the power of our imaginations, we can take the same event and extend it into a happy ending or a disastrous one.

Sometimes the power of thought even makes us live through things that never happened. Have you ever gotten really mad at someone for something you thought they did—and then discovered they didn't do it at all? Have you ever been convinced that you'd been turned down for a job or diagnosed with some terrible illness—only to learn that the worst had not occurred? You may have spent a day or two suffering needless torment—all because of the incredible power of thought.

When Senn Delaney was considering being acquired by a larger organization many years ago, we went through a period when our people's emotions were roiling based on their thoughts about what *might* happen if the deal went through. Half of our employees were excited about the added opportunities the merger would bring—increased sales leads, broader capabilities, and added investments that could help us grow faster. The other half were so sure that we'd lose our unique culture that they were practically in mourning, thinking about updating their résumés and seeking new jobs as refugees from the company they'd "lost." Each group was creating a movie about the future and then reacting to it—all based on little more than the thoughts in their heads.

In the end, that deal didn't take place, and the movie scripts disappeared overnight, replaced by familiar reality. Interestingly, a number of years later we did decide to join a larger firm, Heidrick & Struggles. By then we had trained all of our people to better understand the power of thought and the Mood Elevator, and the transition went smoothly—because no one was distracted by thought-driven mood swings.

Understanding the power of thought to shape your moods can help you control your responses—just as you do when you watch a real movie: You sit in the darkened theater, caught up in the drama and the suspense; the music is playing, and the special effects are making your adrenaline flow. But consciously you know it's just a movie. You know that, if it gets too scary, you can take a break to buy some popcorn; and even if the story is tragic, you know you'll return to your normal life when the picture ends.

When you learn to treat your mental movies in that way, your thinking will begin to have less power over you. You will never let go of your moods completely, but knowing that your thoughts are the source of those moods can provide a little added distance and help you remain in control. It's a powerful first step to learning to ride up the Mood Elevator rather than feeling like a helpless victim of emotional forces you can't control—one of a number of steps you'll learn about in the following chapters.

3

Up the Mood Elevator: The Big Payoffs

We are formed and molded by our thoughts.
Those whose minds are shaped by selfless thoughts
give joy when they speak or act. Joy follows
them like a shadow that never leaves them.

—GAUTAMA BUDDHA

As we saw in chapter 2, thought plays a major role in controlling our travels up and down the Mood Elevator. Our thoughts influence all the feelings we experience, from joy to depression. Understanding that our thinking creates our emotional reality is the first step in taking control.

Knowing that our thoughts control our moods gives us a little distance from those moods. It helps us be less gripped by worry, fear, and anxiety and less driven by our emotions to pronounce judgments on other people and on the circumstances of our lives.

This understanding is the first basic principle of riding the Mood Elevator. And it is so powerful that it can have—and has had for thousands of people—a series of enormous payoffs, both in your personal life and in your ability to contribute to any organization to which you belong.

The Personal Payoffs

The payoffs you gain from understanding the power of thought begin with a better moment-to-moment experience of life. When you are no longer buffeted by the winds of moods you don't understand and can't control, you'll find that you can enjoy life much more, with a greater sense of peace and freedom. But the benefits go far beyond that. Learning to control your travels on the Mood Elevator can also help you have a more successful career, a more fulfilling job, a more loving marriage, and healthier relationships. In short, it can help you achieve more success with less stress in your life. This is because when we are up the Mood Elevator, we experience higher-quality thinking. Our thinking is clearer, better focused, more organized, and more flowing.

Think about the last time you felt really rushed, frustrated, bothered, or extremely impatient, with nothing going quite right. It might have been a time when you were late for an important meeting, struggling to finish a complicated project, or dealing with an emergency that was just beyond your competence level.

Recall what your thinking is like in these situations. If it's like mine, it is probably very scattered and unfocused. The morning when I am under the most intense pressure to get to a meeting on time is precisely when I am most likely to misplace something important—like my keys or phone. It's also the time when I'm most likely to fumble seemingly simple tasks. My thoughts race, and answering even basic questions or solving easy problems seems difficult. The same result can occur whenever I get overly excited, emotional, or intense.

The fact is that just as our thoughts drive the Mood Elevator, our travels on the Mood Elevator in turn have a profound effect on the quality of our thinking.

When we are down the Mood Elevator, we suffer from lower-quality thinking. Our thoughts are often circular, going around and around in the same cycle of emotions and feelings driven by anxiety, uncertainty, and confusion. Our thinking is busy and more cluttered. We don't make sense of our environment as well as we usually do. We aren't as tuned in to other people, what is on their minds, or the impact we are having on them.

By contrast, have you ever found yourself wrestling fruitlessly with a complicated problem only to discover that when you let it go, a creative solution occurs to you? Our thinking improves when we travel up the Mood Elevator. This often happens to us when we relax, quiet our mind, change our pattern of thinking, and escape the grip of anxiety—perhaps by exercising, taking a walk, or listening to music. Even a routine chore like vacuuming the house or mowing the lawn can be helpful. In fact, one study found that people reported having the most new, creative ideas while taking a shower! The sound, rhythm, and warmth of the water blocks out the world and the internal noises generated by our thoughts, permitting our quieter minds to return to higher-quality thinking. When we are up the Mood Elevator and have higher-quality thinking, we have full access to the capabilities of our minds.

At times like these, you may feel as though you are "in the zone." Mihaly Csikszentmihalyi, former chairman of the Department of Psychology at the University of Chicago, described this phenomenon in his book *Flow: The Psychology of Optimal Experience.* Csikszentmihalyi found that there are "flow times" that all people have when they are absorbed and in tune with what they are doing. During these flow times, people have exceptionally clear, creative, and resourceful thinking; somehow they are able to discover appropriate ways to tackle any problem they are grappling with. These positive responses seem to come to them naturally and effortlessly.

Crucially, in reflecting on my own life and in thinking about the stories others have shared with me, I've discovered that flow times are strongly related to the moods people experience at the upper levels on the Mood Elevator. This means flow times need not be rare moments in our lives. Although no one is *always* in the zone, a form of flow state can become a habitual way of life—once we learn to travel up the Mood Elevator, not just occasionally and accidentally, but frequently and deliberately.

Reconnecting with your best self. One of my deeply held beliefs and a basic premise of this book is that we all come into this world with the potential for mental and emotional health. Our natural state is to be loving, creative, trusting, forgiving, curious, happy, and desirous of warm, close relationships with others.

We often see this state in very young children. To most youngsters life is a wonder. They are spontaneous and they live in the moment. They get over everyday hurts easily, and they don't hold grudges. They are naturally up the Mood Elevator much of the time. Of course, they sometimes go down the elevator, too. We've all seen children exhibit anger, impatience, and irritation, but kids generally don't stay at the lower levels for long periods as adults may do. In large part this is because children tend to hold their thinking more lightly; they haven't yet decided how things "are supposed to be," so they are open to taking life as it comes, not as their minds interpret it.

Unfortunately, as we grow up most of us develop thought habits or beliefs that can mask or obscure our innate health. At some point we are hurt by someone, and we may become more guarded or defensive. We are criticized for a mistake, and we may learn to make excuses and blame others, seeking to become less accountable so we don't look bad. We play competitive sports, and we may adopt a self-centered win/lose versus win/win mind-set. We are negatively judged for being ourselves, and we may develop an alter ego that is inauthentic. These thought habits can drive us down the Mood Elevator, causing us to lose touch with the healthy child inside us.

Happily, my work as a consultant has shown me that practically everyone retains that childlike health somewhere inside them. They simply need to be reminded of it, encouraged to reconnect with it, and taught simple techniques that will help make that possible. You'll learn many such techniques in this book. As a result, you'll be empowered to rediscover the healthy attitudes of openness, creativity, and joy that most children exhibit—and that also characterize adults at their best.

One time when I was fishing with my son Logan, we were using a bobber—a plastic ball that floats on the water's surface, with the line and bait dangling beneath it. It's called a bobber because you can see it move up and down when a fish starts to nibble on the bait. The fish periodically pulls the bobber underwater, but the bobber's natural state is to pop back up to the surface. In the same way, our natural state is to be up the Mood Elevator. Thoughts of worry, judgment, and insecurity are like the fish—they nibble at us and pull us under temporarily. But when we quiet our minds and let go of those thoughts, our natural health bobs back up.

Maintaining your mental traction. People who lose their cool at times of difficulty, stress, or conflict are at a distinct disadvantage, especially when it comes to dealing with the inappropriate behavior of other people. I've found that if I can keep my composure when someone I am dealing with exhibits impatience, anger, or hostility, I'll almost certainly come out ahead. But when I respond by losing my mental traction, the situation tends to spiral out of control.

Many years ago I saw an illusionist's act at the Universal Studios theme park. The illusionist invited three of the strongest-looking guys in the audience to come onstage, take off their shoes, and stand in a spot he designated.

Next the illusionist asked a petite woman to join them onstage, remove her shoes, and stand on another designated spot about 10 feet from the men. He then gave the men one end of a rope and the woman the other end and asked them to have a tug-of-war. To everyone's amazement, the woman easily pulled the three large men across the floor.

It turned out that the guys had been placed on a spot where the floor was coated with a very slippery space-age material, so they couldn't get any traction in their stocking feet. By contrast, the woman was standing on a rubber pad with lots of traction. With this advantage it didn't take much strength for the woman to move the men.

When we drop several floors down the Mood Elevator—especially without realizing it and adjusting for it—we lose our mental traction. We can't think clearly, communicate well, or react quickly. Under those circumstances, seemingly modest difficulties can easily topple us.

There are simple steps you can take to maintain your own mental traction. Remember the tug-of-war image the next time you are dealing with a difficult person—someone who's thinking has trapped them in a negative, arrogant, aggressive, or defensive mood. Then take a deep breath and consciously embrace thoughts that will enable you to regain the sense of perspective, understanding, and insight you get from traveling up the Mood Elevator. You'll keep your emotional footing and enjoy a far better outcome.

Having access to original ideas. Another reason why we do better when we're on the upper floors is because we have more ready access to the sources of original ideas.

The fact is that most of what goes on in our thinking is not new or creative. We are usually just reprocessing what's already in our memory banks or sorting new input into categories based on what we already know and have experienced. Think about a typical conversation around the water cooler or at a cocktail party. When you mention children, the people you are talking to will tell you about their kids; when you mention vacation, they will recount their last holiday. Similarly, in most business discussions the ideas proposed are familiar ones that break no new ground. In all of these cases, the underlying dynamic is the same: nothing new has entered the system, so nothing particularly creative or original comes out.

There's nothing wrong with reusing what we already know or with sorting new information into preexisting categories. Both are practical uses of our mental capacity. But original ideas come from the highest levels of our minds, where insight and wisdom reside. Some people would say they even come from *beyond* our individual experience—from some form of collective intelligence that we can tap into only under specific circumstances. That's certainly how it *feels* when new, seemingly inexplicable insights pop into our brains.

Original ideas are the source of breakthroughs and inventions—new solutions to old problems and new ways of seeing and doing things. While driving in his 1988 Chevy Blazer on July 4, 1994, a young engineer named Jeff Bezos had just such a novel idea. It occurred to him that the then-fledgling Internet could serve as a distribution system for products to the masses. He pulled over, took out a notepad, and sketched out a business plan for a website to sell books. He named the new business Amazon, after the river with thousands of branches and tributaries, and it led to a retailing revolution.

When we're on the lower floors of the Mood Elevator, original ideas generally elude us. Driven by the negative moods that dominate our minds and emotions, we lose our sense of perspective. The options we perceive as available to us narrow, and our thinking becomes increasingly restricted and memory-based, making us more inclined to cling to the old than to visualize the possibilities of the new. We become less flexible, less resilient, and less open-minded.

By contrast, when we are higher on the Mood Elevator, original ideas are more likely. Few of us have devised new business concepts that revolutionized an industry, but most of us have enjoyed access to original ideas during our moments on the top floors.

Remember that time you were struggling with a project or problem and seeing very few options because your energy was low and you were tired and dispirited? Then you changed your mood—perhaps through something as simple as a good night's sleep, a weekend off, or a change of scenery—and all of a sudden a range of possibilities opened before you. The solution to the problem popped into your brain almost effortlessly. You may have found yourself marveling, *How obvious! I wonder why that didn't occur to me before?* The effects of the Mood Elevator provide an explanation.

Learning to spend more time on the upper floors can give you enhanced access to the creative, innovative capabilities of your mind. The more you cultivate this phenomenon in your life and work, the more success and less stress you'll tend to experience.

The Organizational Payoffs

Learning to ride the Mood Elevator offers huge benefits for the individual, but it also offers major payoffs for organizations whose employees practice this skill. It's no accident that many of Senn Delaney's clients who teach their employees about the Mood Elevator have appeared on *Fortune*'s list of most admired companies, won J.D. Power awards for best customer service, and earned high rankings on the employee engagement scores measured by the Gallup polling organization.

One of the core beliefs that guides our culture-shaping work at Senn Delaney is that, in a fundamental sense, we don't have to *teach* our clients anything; we just give them practical ways to reconnect with the best of who they already are. That happens naturally for people and organizations when they are up the Mood Elevator. When leaders and teams operate at their best, their innately healthy behaviors are enhanced, and organizations flourish.

I've already noted that most people, as they grow up, gradually lose the natural mental and emotional health that characterizes many young children. Instead they learn thought habits that make them vulnerable to negative attitudes and behaviors like fear, defensiveness, and inauthenticity. Many of these learned habits show up as dysfunctions in the organizations they join. Win/lose political conflicts and lack of trust cause needless rifts and misunderstandings. Departments and individuals blame one another and engage in battles over power, prestige, and resources. As a result, organizations waste time, energy, and money struggling to overcome personal and cultural dysfunctions rather than focusing on productivity, creativity, and growth.

When we perform the Senn Delaney cultural diagnostics with a new client company, the resulting Corporate Culture Profile often yields scores that indicate problem areas. One of the scores most often found in the red zone, indicating serious dysfunction, is employees' not feeling valued and appreciated. That is not surprising. These days most organizations operate at a faster pace than ever before—often dismissing the human dimension. But that's a recipe for trouble because it leads to a lack of employee engagement and a poor customer experience.

Fortunately, we are able to use the concepts in this book to consistently move our clients out of the red zone and toward a healthy, high-performing culture with more positive energy and spirit. It is empowering for our clients to learn that they can return to the productive forms of thinking, feeling, and behaving that elude them when they are down the Mood Elevator—*and* that they can be highly productive and have employees and customers who feel valued and appreciated. Our clients learn that healthy organizational behaviors are only a thought away—and they learn how to access them.

Values that move an organization up the Mood Elevator. Senn Delaney's work in an organization generally includes a customized off-site session with the CEO and his or her senior team. Toward the end of the session, after discussing and experiencing the modes of behavior they consider most enjoyable, productive, and rewarding, the team members usually find themselves at the top levels of the Mood Elevator, feeling and operating at their best. At that moment we ask them to define how they want to relate to one another once they are back in the office—and how they want to apply the same style of interaction throughout the organization. In response, the leadership team compiles a list of values that define a healthy, high-performing culture.

The Essential Organizational Values

Attitudes and Behaviors Found
up the Mood Elevator

▶ The foundation: a positive, optimistic spirit based on respect, trust, recognition, and caring (as opposed to pessimism, cynicism, and mistrust)

▶ Personal accountability and an intense desire for excellence (as opposed to blaming and excuses)

▶ Mutually supportive relationships and teamwork dedicated to the benefit of the entire organization (as opposed to selfishness, turf battles, and win/ lose political conflict)

▶ Curiosity and an open, learning mind-set supported by encouragement for risk taking and innovation (as opposed to judgment and resistance to new ideas)

▶ Integrity, authenticity, and transparency (as opposed to pretense and secrecy)

▶ A purposeful connection to and focus on the organization's highest cause or reason for existence (as opposed to cynicism and self-interest)

Over time, having undergone this process with hundreds of organizations, we noticed obvious similarities among the lists of values they developed. We concluded that any group in a healthy place—higher on the Mood Elevator—tends to gravitate toward the same fundamental attitudes and behaviors. We compiled these into a list of what we call the Essential Organizational Values. It comprises all the behaviors that come naturally to people on the higher floors of the Mood Elevator but elude them when they are on the lower floors. We've found that the most successful teams and organizations live these essential values better than others. As a result, the individuals who belong to these groups usually find that they can spend more time on the penthouse floor, and they are happier, more creative, and more productive as a result.

Some companies embody the Essential Organizational Values better than others, but practically every leadership team that takes time for self-reflection recognizes their importance and aspires to live by them. The same values have risen to the surface consistently in our work in more than 50 countries with groups ranging from 100-plus CEO teams of Fortune 500 companies to teams of state governors and university presidents. We believe that the Essential Organizational Values represent universal principles of life effectiveness for individuals as well as organizations.

It is fascinating to see how these principles play out in organizations. One example is L Brands, the parent company of the popular retail chains Bath & Body Works and Victoria's Secret. The Essential Organizational Values show up at L Brands under the rubric of The L Brand Way—the company's own definition of the culture it aspires to cultivate.

In an era when many business organizations have come under fire for unethical behaviors, L Brands has made a fundamental commitment to living its values, not just pursuing profit. In the words of company founder and CEO Les Wexner, business is not just about winning: "It matters how you play the game."[2] *Fortune* magazine named L Brands one of the Most Admired Retailers in the world. The company was also recognized by the Center for Effective Organizations at the University of Southern California as one of the most agile in the United States.

When employees of many of the world's best companies were surveyed, L Brands was ranked highest in several crucial metrics:

▶ "Decisions and actions reflect customer care."

▶ "I feel valued as an associate."

▶ "I have the opportunity to develop the skills I need to be successful in the future."

▶ "It is easy for people of diverse backgrounds to fit in—and be accepted."

In explaining these achievements, Wexner commented, "It is our thinking driving our behaviors and our results"—the language of riding the Mood Elevator applied to organizational achievement.

Another CEO who has employed the power of the Mood Elevator to enhance his organization's performance is David Novak of YUM! Brands, which manages 36,000 KFC, Pizza Hut, and Taco Bell restaurants and 1.7 million employees around the world. YUM! Brands has effectively used the Mood Elevator as a tool to shape its culture and the employee and customer experience. YUM! Brands is one of a handful of large global companies that hold the distinction of a decade of annual earnings growth exceeding 10 percent, and Novak was named CEO of the Year by *Chief Executive* magazine for his accomplishments.

Novak's best-selling book, *Taking People with You: The Only Way to Make Big Things Happen,* includes a section on the Mood Elevator. In a *CEO Show* interview, Novak observed, "The worst thing you can do is go to work every day and not have a positive attitude. You've got to at least move yourself up the Mood Elevator and get in the 'curious and interested' level to be an effective leader—and you make your best decisions at the top when you are grateful."[3]

A third leader who has used the Mood Elevator as a leadership tool is General Josue "Joe" Robles Jr., former CEO of USAA, the military insurance and financial services company. A much-decorated officer, Robles was named Innovator of the Year in 2009 by *American Banker* magazine, and under his leadership USAA was repeatedly ranked number one among all US companies in surveys on customer service and customer loyalty. Robles uses the Mood Elevator to bring out the best in people and teams. As he says, "The concept has been invaluable in all walks of life for people at USAA. It helps us work better together as business colleagues but has equal benefit in personal relationships."[4]

Robles retired from USAA in 2015 and was promptly asked by President Barack Obama to serve as chair of the Department of Veterans Affairs' newly formed MyVA Advisory Committee, with the mission of making the VA more effective and accessible to the veterans it is intended to serve.

Fewer organizations today are neglecting issues of culture, values, and attitudes. Those that do are driven by thinking that "soft" topics are less meaningful and significant than traditional "hard" factors like strategy and systems. But our experience with organizations in every industry and country has shown that it's the soft stuff that largely determines success in life and in organizations. That's why learning to master the Mood Elevator offers such big payoffs for companies that wisely devote some time and energy to self-reflection.

∾

In chapter 4 we delve further into the secrets of riding the Mood Elevator—beginning with the challenge of recognizing and understanding your own moods so that you can take steps to deliberately alter and control them.

Escaping Unhealthy Normal

Change your thoughts and you change your world.

—Norman Vincent Peale

Once we understand that our thinking creates our moods, we still face a problem: we can generally justify our thinking no matter how unreasonable it may be. Recall how John in chapter 1 came up with seemingly logical evidence to support his feelings about his job at Tip-Top Products, even as those feelings veered wildly from positive to negative and back again. The fact is that our thinking does not serve as a very trustworthy guide to how we are doing in life. If you simply listen to your thinking, you'll likely remain stuck on whatever floor on the Mood Elevator your thoughts delivered you to in the first place.

But there is good news. Fortunately, we human beings are endowed with not only the gift of thought but also the gift of emotion. Each thought provokes a feeling, and every feeling we experience is a signal about how we are relating to the world. In a sense, the Mood Elevator is just a "feelings barometer"—a sensitive instrument that reflects the varying state of our emotions from high to low. So when you want to know how you are doing, look to your feelings as your guide. They can provide meaningful clues to the reliability of your thinking and the impact it is having, not only on you but on those around you, as well.

Learning to Read Your Human Dashboard

The big news in autos today is electronics. The dashboards in new cars feature an amazing array of information, from engine warning signals to tire pressure. The Mood Elevator is your human dashboard. The moods you experience can let you know how things are working inside you, at levels of emotion you may find difficult to understand or analyze.

Just as a red light on your car's dashboard starts blinking when the engine is overheating, rising anger offers a warning when your emotions start heating up. And just as your car's gas gauge warns you when you are low on fuel, the feelings of apathy and depression let you know when your emotional energy level is at a low ebb. And just as your GPS navigation system announces "Recalculating!" when you make a wrong turn, feelings like frustration and anxiety can alert you when you are on the wrong path and need to reevaluate your direction.

That's one important purpose of the Mood Elevator: it acts like a human dashboard to let you know how you are doing. If you can learn to notice your feelings as they change—particularly when you find yourself slipping toward the lower floors—you can allow those warnings to trigger corrective actions, following the pointers in this book. This will help you spend more time living up the Mood Elevator—and at your best.

Over time you'll become sensitively attuned to the blinking lights and warning signs that alert you when you are drifting down to the lower levels—especially when the floor is a familiar one that you've visited many times.

My most common lower floor is impatience. I experience it in a variety of ways, some of which may be familiar to you as well:

> *Why is this darned traffic moving so poorly?*

> *Of course, the checkout line I chose turns out to be the slowest—and now the customer in front of me is arguing about a 50-cent coupon!*

> *Why is it taking so long for my computer to boot up?*

> *Come on, people—we've talked about this business issue for 30 minutes. Let's just make a decision!*

I've learned to recognize the emotions that accompany impatience. I feel tense, a little irritated, even a bit "bottled up." If the feeling lasts for more than a few minutes, it can easily morph into anger. And it often leads to foolish choices: I make an irritable remark to the cashier, who is doing her best to handle the line of customers, or I rush to conclude a business discussion before all the facts have been fully evaluated.

Worry is another familiar lower floor to me. It comes with its own set of feelings—usually not as intense as anger but sometimes even more unsettling. I most often recognize worry by noticing that the stories I am creating in my thoughts are going around and around in circles—and with each revolution the imaginary outcome gets worse and worse. If I don't take steps to stop the worry cycle, a small source of concern can become a major drama.

One recurring cycle for me has to do with my passion for physical fitness. I'm driven to keep in shape because of my deep-seated belief that fitness improves mood and mental well-being. For me there is nothing like a morning jog to clear my mind and start the day up the Mood Elevator. It is also when I get my most creative original thoughts and solve problems. I've been blessed to be able to jog decades longer than most people, whose knees go by their sixties. For many years now, every time I feel even minor knee pain while running, I have to be on guard or my thinking can weave a disaster scenario: *Maybe my knees are finally going. Then I can't run anymore and I won't be as creative. I won't be able to stay in shape by training for triathlons. Without cardio exercise, my longevity could be affected.*

Awareness is the key to reading your human dashboard. Carrying a Mood Elevator pocket card as a handy reminder helps keep that awareness front of mind. Learning to read the signals your feelings evoke is important because the first step in managing mood states is knowing which one you are in.

Unfortunately, we all run the risk of becoming boiled frogs when it comes to habitual emotional states. Think about a time when you found yourself routinely bothered or irritated by people and events—perhaps when you were working in an organization suffering from some dysfunctional behavior patterns. Hopefully, you remedied the problem by changing either your circumstances or the thoughts you embraced in response to those circumstances. But if you didn't, you may have found yourself gradually becoming more and more bothered until the state of irritation was so familiar you no longer even noticed it.

Eventually, a mood of impatience, frustration, and pessimism became your unhealthy normal. You may have gone through life unaware of your habitual unhappiness until something external brought it to your attention—perhaps an encounter with an old friend who remarked, "Wow, what's eating you? You never used to walk around with a scowl like that on your face!"

There are many manifestations of unhealthy normal. At one point in my life, my unhealthy normal was excessive intensity. I was overly concerned about getting everything done, doing everything right, meeting every deadline, never disappointing anyone, and being successful at everything I did. I was continuously wound up. Except for those relatively rare times when I took a real break—such as a long vacation—I didn't even remember that it was possible to experience a calmer, more peaceful existence.

For others, habitual states of insecurity, judgment, worry, blaming, anger, or depression may become their unhealthy normal. The problem, of course, is that if you don't notice your state of unhealthy normal, you won't be prompted to do anything about it. A habitual mood can become a self-destructive way of life.

Thankfully, there is something you can do. The key is to make a continuous, conscious effort to pay attention to your feelings by reading your own dashboard and reacting appropriately.

Sometimes recognizing a state of unhealthy normal requires being sensitive to external cues—like a driver who doesn't realize he has a burned-out headlight until another driver alerts him to the trouble.

In my case it was promptings from family, colleagues, and friends that made me realize that excessive intensity had become my unhealthy normal. I set to work to recognize when my overly driven nature was giving rise to feelings of impatience, anxiety, and irritation. In time my sensitivity increased until those emotions became like a loud bell that I found impossible to ignore. I developed the habit of taking a deep breath and saying to myself, *There you go again! It's time to escape from that mood of excessive intensity. Be calm. Be present. And take life just a little easier.* Over time my periods of excessive intensity greatly diminished.

We are all gifted with a personal dashboard that can save us from the worst mood disorders—but it won't do you any good unless you read it. Pay attention to the signals you get, internally and externally, and learn to be a sensitive monitor of the emotional gauges on your human dashboard.

Unhealthy Normal and Relationships

When my wife's parents used to come visit us, she and I would notice how much they bickered. They would disagree about the most inconsequential things and constantly make each other wrong through subtle put-downs or sarcastic shots. They were oblivious to their continuous state of hostility; it had become their unhealthy normal, and they didn't notice it or see anything wrong with their relationship.

My in-laws aren't alone in this pattern of behavior; destructive, unhealthy-normal mood states often arise in long-term relationships. Couples start to take each other for granted, stop communicating appreciation for each other, and gradually lose touch with their feelings of love and affection.

There's no sphere of life in which paying attention to your feelings is more important than in close relationships. The feelings to watch for and cultivate are love, appreciation, forgiveness, nonjudgment, and compassion. When you keep these feelings alive, relationships flourish. When you stop monitoring your emotions, an unhealthy normal may develop, in which judgment, faultfinding, resentment, grudge holding, and bitterness take root.

George Pransky and his wife, Linda, head a counseling practice for individuals and organizations based in the state of Washington. They often work with couples to help them understand the three principles of *mind, thought,* and *consciousness* that they consider central to healthy relationships. Sydney Banks, who helped formulate the three principles, defines them as "Mind, which is the source of all intelligence, Consciousness, which allows us to be aware of our existence, and Thought, which guides us through the world we live in as free-thinking agents." Pransky teaches the concept that "consciousness makes thought appear real to each person in the moment, and therefore individual reality is created via the medium of personal mindsets and thinking."[5] You might notice that this is a philosophical version of the ideas presented in this book.

George Pransky tells the story of a couple who came for a four-day residential retreat because they felt that love was leaving their marriage. He helped them see that habitual practices of arguing, fighting, and making each other wrong had become their unhealthy normal.

Uplifted by this new insight, the couple left the retreat in a loving and hopeful state, but a week later George got a panicked call from the husband. "We've failed," he announced. "We just had a fight, and we are both so upset that we did."

George replied, "Congratulations! You *noticed* this time, and you didn't like it. That's the best thing that could have happened." The couple's undesirable behaviors and accompanying feelings had become a loud bell that they couldn't help but notice—the first and most important step toward positive, lasting change.

Unhealthy Normal in Organizations

In Senn Delaney's work with corporate clients, our goal is to inspire, educate, and partner with them to foster healthy, high-performing organizational cultures. When we run a set of cultural diagnostics, we almost always discover some behaviors and attitudes that are hindering them from achieving the positive, creative, productive state to which they aspire. It takes an outsider to see these dysfunctions clearly because people who have been together for a while develop what could be called *familiarity blindness*—an organizational form of unhealthy normal.

Sometimes unhealthy-normal habits develop in an organization as a result of deliberate choices by the company's leaders.

One of the most extreme examples is the story of Enron, the energy and commodities trading firm based in Houston, Texas, that back in the 1990s was widely admired as one of the world's most creative, unconventional—and seemingly profitable—companies. *Fortune* named Enron "America's most innovative company" an unparalleled six years in a row.

In the midst of this remarkable run of success, I was asked to meet with Enron's top executives, who were interested in exploring ways that Senn Delaney could help them foster an even more successful culture. Our team quickly realized that Enron's culture was driven entirely by an excessive focus on self-interest. We pointed this out and warned the company's leaders that, in the long run, this approach to business carried significant dangers and was ultimately unsustainable. But they told us they wanted even more of what they already had—a culture centered on extremely high performance expectations permeated with an every-person-for-themselves, dog-eat-dog, results-at-any-cost mind-set.

We turned down the engagement. A few years later, in late 2001, the company collapsed, embroiled in one of the most gigantic cases of corporate fraud in history. Subsequent accounts revealed that Enron had pushed—and exceeded—the limits of integrity and ethics in search of ways to maintain its string of increased quarterly earnings. The few people within Enron who understood what was happening and tried to call it out became social outcasts, thanks to the unhealthy-normal behavior pervasive throughout the organization.

Granted, Enron is an extreme example, but a lack of collaboration coupled with excessive self-interest is perhaps the most common dysfunctional organizational habit. Senn Delaney saw that early on in our work to help transform the culture of the regional Bell telephone companies after the giant AT&T divestiture in 1982.

Bell Atlantic, composed of state phone companies on the Eastern Seaboard, was our first telecom client. Its CEO, Ray Smith, knew he needed to quickly convert a monopolistic, state-centric company into a collaborative global competitor, and he called on Senn Delaney to help.

We recognized that we had a challenge on our hands when Bell Atlantic employees told us that it was common for workers in one state phone company division to celebrate if another state phone company lost a rate case with the local regulators, even though this hurt the company's profits. "When they lose, it makes us look better by comparison!" they explained. A friendly rivalry among members of the same organization may help encourage hard work and creativity, but when it causes people to rejoice at the misfortunates of colleagues and partners, it's a sign that the culture has gone badly awry.

Another dysfunctional organizational habit that is all too common is the blame game. We are taught from childhood—thanks in part to sports and games—that for me to win, you have to lose. That dynamic shows up in organizations as well as in families and couples, where it takes the form of one person needing to be right while making the other wrong. When that becomes an unconscious habit, organizations suffer and marriages can end.

Early in our work developing Senn Delaney's culture-shaping model, our retail consulting group was doing some projects for the JL Hudson department stores in Detroit, then part of the Dayton Hudson retail giant and now part of Macy's. One assignment was to improve the dismal performance of the company's Warren Distribution Center, where goods were received from vendors, checked, marked, sorted, and then sent off to the stores.

After a thorough study of the center's operations, we couldn't find anything wrong with its layout, equipment, systems, or processes, but our interviews revealed an almost terminal case of lack of accountability. Everyone said there was a problem—but then pointed to someone else as the cause of it. The markers blamed the checkers, the checkers blamed the buyers, the buyers blamed the vendors, and the venders blamed the markers.

In a leadership session with the distribution team, we surfaced their blame-game mentality and replaced it with a mind-set of accountability. This paved the way for across-the-board improvement in business practices over time. Eventually, the Warren Distribution Center was transformed from the worst to the best performer in the Dayton Hudson group.

Heeding the Warning Signs

How can you recognize when dysfunctional attitudes and behaviors have become your unhealthy normal? Check your Mood Elevator and use your feelings as your guide—so long as those feelings haven't themselves become an unhealthy normal. If that's the case, you need to relearn to recognize your lower-floor emotions. Start by seeing whether you can identify any unhealthy-normal tendencies you might have:

▶ Impatience

▶ Pessimism

▶ Irritation

▶ Anger

▶ Anxiety

▶ Worry

▶ Excessive intensity

▶ A judgmental attitude

▶ Insecurity

▶ A sense of unworthiness

▶ Neediness

▶ The need to be right

▶ Argumentativeness

▶ Self-righteousness

▶ Disconnection

▶ Blaming or excuses

▶ An unwillingness to admit mistakes

Pay attention to these feelings when you experience them; listen carefully for external cues that can alert you to their presence. If friends, associates, or family members start dropping hints that they have detected in you the attitudes or behaviors associated with these emotions, don't dismiss them. Take them seriously; they are trying to tell you that your human dashboard is flashing warning lights—signs that you have been overlooking.

Once you start to recognize the unhealthy patterns of behavior in your life, learning to catch—and respond to—the feelings associated with those patterns can be extremely useful. We explore ways to do that in later chapters.

Braking Your Mood Elevator: The Power of Curiosity

The highest form of human intelligence is to observe yourself without judgment.

—JIDDU KRISHNAMURTI

Throughout this book we've been using the metaphor of the Mood Elevator to describe how our emotions rise and fall. But of course there are countless *real* elevators in use around the world every day. Experts say that passengers take more than 18 *billion* elevator trips annually in the United States alone. Why is it that you never hear about elevators plummeting to the basement? That only happens in horror movies and nightmares because, in addition to being safely built and inspected, all modern elevators have a series of automatic brakes that prevent them from falling, even if a cable snaps. Thanks to this ingenious system (invented by

Elisha Otis back in 1852), riding in an elevator is actually far safer than taking the stairs.

In a similar way, you can learn to activate a brake on your Mood Elevator. There's an automatic system designed by nature to catch you before your emotional state falls too far and too quickly—provided you choose to employ it.

Look back at the Mood Elevator map in chapter 1. Where would you draw a line between the higher states and the lower states?

The dividing line is "curious, interested." It appears right in the middle of the map, and it serves as an ideal braking point before you drop to the lower mood states. Living life with more curiosity is a great way to avoid dropping to the lower floors. Here's how it works.

When something happens that threatens to make you plunge to the bottom on the Mood Elevator—for example, when someone says or does something you disagree with or fail to understand—you can choose to be irritated, distressed, or judgmental. You can respond by thinking, *What a stupid thing to do! That just ruined my whole day! They must be trying to get my goat!* You'll immediately feel your emotions pulling your Mood Elevator to the basement.

On the other hand, you can choose to be curious. You can respond by thinking, *I wonder why they did that. What an unusual and surprising thing to do. It would be interesting to understand what caused them to act that way.*

When life throws you a curve, you can become angry, depressed, or defensive—or you can put your energy into learning from the situation and developing creative ways to comprehend and respond to it. This requires a curious mind. The ultimate outcome will vary, but you will always be further ahead if you begin with curiosity.

Resisting Your Emotional Impulses

To understand why curiosity can serve as a brake on your Mood Elevator, look at the following paragraph. What kinds of thoughts and emotions does it trigger in you?

> Those taht raed tihs hvae a sgtrane mnid. Olny 55 plepoe out of 100 can. I cdnuolt blveiee that I cluod aulaclty uesdnatnrd what I was rdanieg. The pha-onmneal pweor of the hmuan mind. Aoccdrnig to rscheearch at Cmabrigde Uinervtisy, it dseno't mtaetr in what oerdr the ltteres in a word are, the olny iproamtnt tihng is that the frsit and last ltteer be in the rghit pclae. The rset can be a taotl mses and you can still raed it whotuit a pboerlm. This is bcuseae the huamn mnid deos not raed ervey lteter idnidivaluly but the wrod as a wlohe.

It is certainly an odd-looking paragraph. Did you try to read it? If so, were you able to make sense of it? If the readers of this book are typical, only about half of you will be able to read the paragraph.

More important, what kinds of thoughts and emotions did you experience? Did you find the paragraph's jumbled letters confusing and irritating? Did you quickly give up on trying to read it? Did you find yourself thinking, *What a stupid exercise! How am I supposed to figure out this nonsense?* or *This is a big waste of time.*

If you responded like that, you are like many people. Lots of us tend to react to events that are confusing and upsetting by quickly dropping to one of the most popular floors on the Mood Elevator—the one near the bottom: *judgmental/blaming.*

Now go back to that odd paragraph and try reading it again. You may find it helpful to start with the last sentence first. Take the paragraph slowly, one sentence at a time. Little by little the words and ideas may gradually fall into place.

If that doesn't work, take a look at the same paragraph with the words spelled correctly:

> Those that read this have a strange mind. Only 55 people out of 100 can. I could not believe I could actually understand what I was reading. The phenomenal power of the human mind. According to research at Cambridge University, it doesn't matter in what order the letters in a word are, the only important thing is that the first and last letter be in the right place. The rest can be a total mess and you can still read it without a problem. This is because the human mind does not read every letter individually but the word as a whole.

This example is based on a scientific study investigating how the mind works. Our ability to correctly interpret oddly spelled words is an interesting psychological curiosity that may not seem important in itself—but the way you reacted to the exercise has significant implications.

If you reacted with annoyance and irritation, you've vividly experienced how our Mood Elevators often work. When unusual or surprising events happen, thwarting our expectations and posing difficulties we're unprepared for, we tend to experience uncontrolled emotional responses that quickly carry us to the lower levels.

On the other hand, you may have responded with curiosity. This could have taken several forms, such as a strong desire to unravel the meaning of the paragraph, wondering about the purpose of the unexpected exercise, or perhaps a sense of humorous puzzlement as you gradually untangled a word here, a word there, and slowly discerned the ideas behind entire sentences.

If this was your reaction, congratulations! You see how curiosity can help save you from falling to the bottom levels of your Mood Elevator—while also providing you with an attitude that is tremendously valuable for disentangling many of the knotty challenges that life throws our way.

Here Comes the Judge

Many people tend to respond to experiences that are new and different by swiftly traveling to the Mood Elevator floor labeled *judgmental/blaming*.

It's important to distinguish "being judgmental" from the simple, necessary act of judgment. Of course, we all make judgments every day—about how we will behave, what we will or will not do, tasks or projects we will undertake, how we will tackle problems, and so on. But being judgmental is another matter; it's about *rushing to judgment* by quickly condemning things, ideas, or people that are unfamiliar or challenging, without taking the time to learn about them or even think about them.

There are a number of reasons why being judgmental can be tempting.

Being judgmental relieves us of the hard work of trying to understand something that is unfamiliar. It lets us quickly categorize it according to a simplistic, superficial standard, which is much faster and easier—although the results are often incorrect and ultimately unhelpful.

Being judgmental gives us the pleasurable sensation of being "right" and labeling others as "wrong"—although it often leads to misunderstandings and conflicts that end up causing us more pain than pleasure.

Being judgmental allows us to retain beliefs, concepts, and images of the world that are familiar and comfortable—although it also limits our ability to expand our minds, experience new things, and grow in wisdom and understanding.

Our tendency to judge is why we get into heated arguments with people—including colleagues, friends, and loved ones—about things that really don't matter. It is why so many people are prone to see what is *wrong* with anything that is new or different rather than what is *right* about it—or what can be learned from it. Our tendency to rush to judgment rather than exercise our natural sense of curiosity is the cause of many strained relationships. It's a major reason why most organizations are not as agile or creative as they could be.

Practically everyone is capable of falling into the trap of being judgmental in certain situations. Consider these hypothetical ones:

▶ Your boss announces that the company has chosen a new software system to manage all of your operations at work—and learning how to use it will require two days of training and studying a 100-page manual.

▶ Over dinner your spouse presents you with plans to travel to a new vacation spot that is completely different from the one you love best.

▶ A new colleague at work has a background that is very different from yours; perhaps she's from another country and has a unique education and career path. You're told, "Meet your new partner!"

▶ A family member—a child, a sibling, a parent— informs the family that he or she is making a dramatic life change: a new career, a marriage, a move to a distant state.

▶ Your company announces a merger with a rival firm whose methods, values, and culture are quite different—and you are one of the employees chosen to move to the new operation.

Can you imagine how you might respond, intellectually and emotionally, to one of these situations? You may even have felt yourself reacting with anxiety, irritation, and fear simply from reading these brief descriptions. If so, you can understand why people tend to respond to new challenges with a judgmental attitude, rather than suspend judgment in favor of a spirit of curiosity, openness, and discovery.

Even the most inventive, creative people can fall prey to the tendency to make snap judgments rather than keep an open mind. Back in 2007, Microsoft CEO Steve Ballmer was proudly introducing Vista, a new operating system for personal computers. During an interview with *USA Today,* Ballmer was asked about a new product being released around the same time by high-tech rival Apple. Ballmer didn't hesitate to offer a sweeping judgment about the competition's product: "There's no chance that the iPhone is going to get any significant market share. No chance."[6]

Of course, Ballmer couldn't have been more wrong. Vista was a massive flop, while the iPhone quickly dominated the world of smartphones, revolutionizing the industry and making billions of dollars for Apple.

It's easy to see why Ballmer chose the path of judgment. He was CEO of one of the world's largest and most successful corporations, a company that had pioneered many of the greatest breakthroughs in software; how could his assumptions and beliefs about what customers wanted be wrong? It seemed obvious to Ballmer that no one would want a phone without a keypad—much less that people would use such a phone to surf the Internet, edit videos, listen to music, and play games. The iPhone simply didn't fit Ballmer's image of the world, so he rejected it—rather than study it with an attitude of curiosity, interest, and exploration.

Microsoft's CEO would have been better off gathering his best engineers, designers, and marketing experts around a table; passing around a few of the new iPhones; and asking, "What's new and different about this gadget? Why do you think Apple chose to eliminate the keypad? What new possibilities does this design allow? How do you suppose people will use the iPhone for more than calls and texts? Are there new products or services we could offer that would fit into the iPhone strategy? Is there anything we can do to take the iPhone concept and make it even better?"

The answers to questions like these might have generated a lot of fresh, innovative thinking at Microsoft—and saved the company from having to play catchup to Apple for the next several years.

Choose Curiosity

You can choose to view life with curiosity. When life throws you a curveball—when things happen that are unexpected, confusing, unpleasant, disruptive, or painful—you can follow the path of your immediate emotional impulses, become judgmental, and head toward the lower floors on the Mood Elevator. Or you can take a deep breath, step back from your negative emotional responses, and choose to be curious. Ask yourself:

▶ What's the underlying cause behind this surprising, disturbing event?

▶ What is motivating this behavior that I find so difficult to understand?

▶ What can I learn from this unusual happening?

▶ How can I make something positive out of this apparently negative occurrence?

▶ How might I need to grow or change?

When clients attending Senn Delaney's culture-shaping sessions ask, "What's the single most important takeaway from your program?" I usually respond, "Choose to live life in curiosity rather than judgment. If you do, you'll have more satisfying relationships and a more successful, less stressful life."

Make the curiosity floor on the Mood Elevator your best friend. Visit it often and reap the remarkable benefits it offers. You'll find yourself spending a lot more time in the penthouse and a lot less time in the basement.

Interrupting Your Pattern

Look at everything as though you are seeing it for the
first time, with eyes of a child, fresh with wonder.

—JOSEPH CORNELL

Because our thinking plays such a crucial role in trigger-
ing our feelings and moods, it follows that if we can change
our thinking, we can often change our mood. It isn't easy,
but there is one technique that sometimes works. It's called
a *pattern interrupt,* and it is simply a way to let go of one
train of thought and switch to another.

What follows is what a pattern interrupt might look
like in everyday life.

Imagine that you are in a low mood, concerned about
something that happened during the day. It might be a difficulty at work, a relationship challenge, or an issue in your
community—let's say, for example, the recent news that a
local reservoir *may* have been contaminated with waste
from a nearby factory.

You've spent the day obsessing about the news, discussing it over the breakfast table with your spouse and

around the water cooler with your colleagues. Driving home from work, you are thinking about it and directing the movie in your mind:

> *Suppose it turns out that the local water supply* has *been polluted—and maybe it has been for the past few years. What does that mean for my health and that of my family? Will one of us develop cancer in the near future? Maybe my kids' brain functioning has been impaired—it could be that their grades are going to suffer. And as the word spreads, property values in our town are sure to fall. We may not be able to sell our house at all! And we have most of our family wealth tied up in our home equity. This could turn out to be a disaster that will affect us for years to come.*

By the time you get home, you're in a state of extreme stress, hostility, and depression. But as you walk in the door, the phone rings. It's your best friend. Just hearing his voice makes you feel better. And what he has to say is even more cheering: "Remember that Broadway show that's coming to town next week? I managed to snag four tickets, and we want the two of you to join us. We'll have dinner first and make it a fun night out. What do you say?"

You and your buddy chat about how great it will be to get together and how excited your spouses will be. Your mood shifts immediately because your thinking has shifted. Later, when thoughts about the water supply return, you find yourself thinking about it in a different way:

Of course, there's no proof yet that the reservoir is pol-
luted. Let's wait and see what the county report shows.
And we haven't heard about any possible health effects.
Nobody in the family has shown any unusual symptoms
so far—knock wood! And if it turns out that there is a
problem with the water supply, there are steps we can
take. We can install a filtration system or use bottled
water. And we're lucky to have access to good medical
care at the clinic here in town. Let's take it one step at
a time.

What happened in this story is a pattern interrupt. In many situations, you can invoke your own pattern interrupt rather than wait passively for one to occur from an external source. Pattern interrupts can take many forms, and you need to discover the kinds of pattern interrupts that work for you.

Varieties of Pattern Interrupts

A good night's sleep is a healthy pattern interrupt that's available to everyone. You've almost certainly experienced the mood-altering power of sleep. After a long, tough day, the world often looks overwhelming, people are irritating, and the answers to the problems you face are not evident. But after you get a good night's sleep, though your circumstances haven't changed, your world looks better, simply because your thinking in the morning is different from how it was the night before.

For me, exercise can be a powerful pattern interrupt. I may be tired and feeling low when I roll out of bed in the morning, but by the end of my daily run I am usually inspired, full of good ideas, and ready to face the world. Scientists tell us that running produces endorphins that create a natural high, but there's more to exercise than that. The rhythmic pace, the music I listen to, the natural scenery flowing by—the combination of these positive stimulants clears my mind and quiets me down. Medical experts and psychologists confirm that chemical and physiological factors have a powerful impact on our thoughts and moods, which is why physical activities that alter our internal chemistry can be great pattern interrupts.

Many other forms of exercise can have the same effect. The intake of oxygen associated with deep breathing does a lot to improve my mood. In fact, just focusing on your breathing can be a mini–pattern interrupt. That's why the breathing techniques associated with meditation and prayer can operate much like exercise in quieting the mind and interrupting any negative patterns you've fallen into. (We delve more deeply into the mind/body connection in chapter 9 and describe some additional self-care techniques you can use to stay on a positive emotional and mental path.)

Moods are also contagious. Studies have shown that if you put a person with a low mood state into a group or meeting, often the mood of the whole group goes down.

Conversely, if you put a person in a high mood state into a gathering, the higher mood state also tends to be contagious.

You can consciously take advantage of the contagious quality of moods. When taking a long road trip for client work, I sometimes feel weary and overwhelmed. When this happens I call my wife. She listens as I talk about my day, and she often shares news about something fun, interesting, or exciting that our kids have done. The longer we talk, the more I feel my spirits rising. Bernadette is my pattern interrupt because I generally catch her positive mood state, particularly when I need it most.

Of course, not everyone can play this kind of positive role in your life. While it is not good to categorize people, especially in a rigid way, there are some people in my life whom I tend to view as energy pumps, while others seem to be energy drains. If I want an uplift, I will try to connect with someone who is already where I want to be on the Mood Elevator. Spending time with people in your life who can raise your spirits can be a pattern interrupt—an automatic mood lifter.

By the same token, I try to minimize the time I spend with people who consistently bring me down—although of course it isn't always possible to avoid them. When I must interact with people who tend to dwell on the lower floors, I hope I can act as an energy pump for them, providing them with a bit of the positive energy they seem to lack.

It's a great life strategy to try to surround yourself, to the extent that you can, with people who have a positive influence on your thinking and moods. That quality is something we select and hire for at Senn Delaney. If you get a chance to meet one of our consultants or teammates from our offices around the world, you'll immediately feel the positive energy they exude.

Self-talk can also make a difference in managing moods. I have used self-talk as a pattern interrupt to break out of my worry habit. As mentioned earlier, I've learned to recognize the onset of worry by the emotions it generates, as well as by the thoughts that start swirling around in my head. (I call these my "mental eddies.") Now, as soon as I notice my thinking beginning to swirl in this unproductive, mood-darkening fashion, I say to myself in a lighthearted way, *There you go again!*

Simply being aware of your emotions and giving your-self gentle reminders about how to deal with them can help you check a negative mood before it has a chance to take hold.

Even kids can learn how to use pattern interrupts to transform their attitudes. When our teenage son, Logan, gets upset, bothered, or stressed, he lets my wife and me know that it's best to leave him alone. We've discovered that it's not productive to try to talk to him when he is in the grip of a lower mood state.

Instead, Logan has devised his own system for dealing with it. He goes into his room, shuts the door, and engages in activities he really enjoys—things he can get lost in that distract him from his lower-level thinking. It may be watching a favorite program or playing a computer game that takes his full concentration. Before long Logan emerges from his room and is the loving, lighthearted son we know and love.

Lots of kids have developed an approach similar to Logan's. The main difference is that Logan has done it consciously and practices it deliberately. I know it's true because I once heard him explain his process to the other kids in his Sunday school class: "When I get real grumpy like that, it's not really me," he said. "I'm afraid I will say things I really don't mean, so I don't want to be around people. When I feel I'm myself again, I come back out and join the family."

Computer games are Logan's pattern interrupt. Yours could be a round of golf, a favorite piece of music, a yoga routine, a few minutes playing with a much-loved pet, or a chat with your favorite relative. Experiment until you discover what works for you—and pull it out of your tool kit whenever you feel the need.

Focusing on a Higher Purpose as a Pattern Interrupt

One powerful way to interrupt a negative pattern of thinking and feeling is to shift your attention to a higher purpose. Escaping from your thoughts about yourself—especially when they are centered on worries, fears, insecurities, and hostilities—and moving into thinking about others and their needs can make your Mood Elevator take a big surge upward, gaining access to higher-level thinking, as well as a deeper sense of peace and optimism.

Your "higher purpose" doesn't have to be a grand one. It just needs to be bigger than yourself—something that makes a positive difference in the world. Here are a few simple examples:

- ▶ Listening to a friend in need and offering support and encouragement without judgment or criticism

- ▶ Contributing time or money to a worthy cause

- ▶ Committing to live a spiritual life and modeling those principles in your daily behavior

- ▶ Coaching a kids' team, serving as a team parent, or helping lead a youth group

- ▶ Mentoring a young person in need of guidance, advice, and help

- ▶ Participating in a charity run or walk in support of a good cause

- ▶ Being an attentive parent—caring for and teaching positive values to your child

- ▶ Volunteering at a local soup kitchen, homeless shelter, emergency hotline, or other community service endeavor

Whenever we get past ourselves and do something for others, we shift our mood and raise our spirits. Because we are spending more time on the higher floors, we become more purposeful, creative, and positive—and end up contributing even more to the world around us. It's a wonderful, self-reinforcing cycle.

When Your Mood Elevator Refuses to Budge

As I've suggested, the list of possible pattern interrupts is infinite. Taking a walk, working out, listening to music, helping a friend or child, reading a book, volunteering for a cause, taking a shower or bath, enjoying a massage, taking a nap, going shopping, stopping to watch a sunset—any of these pattern interrupts can shift your thinking to a higher level. Your job is to experiment until you find the activities that work best for you.

Unfortunately, even the pattern interrupts you enjoy most may sometimes fail to work, which raises the question: *Why is it so difficult to get out of certain low mood states, and what can you do when you are really stuck?*

The basic problem is that our thinking always seems to make sense to us in the moment, even when it doesn't really make sense; supported by self-reinforcing emotions, it seems real and compelling. Furthermore, in many cases a low mood state is related to a real problem or challenge we are facing. As a result, we feel justified in our mood, thinking we have a "right" to feel the way we do. The fact is that riding the Mood Elevator up and down is a seemingly unavoidable part of life. Sometimes we are down—often for no apparent reason.

So, if on occasion your preferred pattern interrupt doesn't make a dent in how you are feeling, the best thing to do is to treat your low mood state like bad weather: Don't fight it; just surrender to being human. Know that, like dark clouds in the sky, your low mood will pass and you will feel better. It has happened before and will happen again. Realizing this will help you put the mood in perspective and get through it, doing as little damage as possible to yourself and others.

In most cases, what hurts us is not so much the bad moods we must sometimes suffer through but rather the serious mistakes we make when we overreact while in such moods.

Feeding the Thoughts You Favor

We become what we think about all day long.

—Ralph Waldo Emerson

There's an old legend of the Cherokee people that explains a conflict that goes on inside all of us. In the story a wise old man is talking with his grandson about life.

"My child," says the grandfather, "there is a battle between two wolves that takes place within each of us. One wolf is evil; it is anger, envy, jealousy, sorrow, regret, worry, greed, arrogance, self-pity, guilt, resentment, lies, false pride, and ego. The other wolf is good; it is joy, peace, love, hope, serenity, wisdom, humility, kindness, benevolence, empathy, generosity, truth, compassion, and faith."

The grandson thinks about this for a minute and then asks, "Which wolf will win?"

His grandfather simply replies, "The one you feed."

We all have thoughts that take us to every level on the Mood Elevator, top to bottom. To experience life to the fullest, we have been given the gift of thought and the feelings that go along with it. The question is: *Which kinds of thoughts do we feed, and which thoughts dominate us as a result?*

Sometimes we visit a particular mood level for just a moment; that's a natural aspect of human nature. But at other times, we choose to camp out on a particular floor for extended periods. That behavior is not helpful, at least not when it's a lower floor.

Feeding Your Negative Thoughts

Remember Deborah from chapter 2? She was a new Senn Delaney consultant who was invited to join me on a sales call with a local utility CEO. The prospect made Deb anxious, which is normal and understandable, but she took that thinking a lot further, creating drama in her head in which the sales call was a disaster, she got fired from her job, her son couldn't go to college, and her family lost their house. This low-level thinking and the accompanying feelings of stress, fear, and despair dominated her life in the days leading up to the meeting.

You remember how it worked out in reality: despite Deb's fears, the sales call went well, and she even got some local consulting work out of it. Her worry had served no purpose.

Deborah's story illustrates how our choices determine the impact of our thoughts. A thought like worry can pass through our mind like a leaf that momentarily flits across our path—or we can nurture it, feed it, and embellish it. In extreme cases, we can turn it into a full-length horror movie replete with special effects and catastrophic consequences.

The point is not that worry is bad per se. When managed properly, it can play an important role. Legitimate concerns about the future—thoughts about things that could go wrong—can be useful in prompting us to be aware of potential dangers, to take action to avoid them, and to have a contingency plan in case the dangers materialize. To the extent that worry motivates concrete action that genuinely improves your life circumstances, it is a valuable friend and ally. But when worry starts you on a long journey in your imagination that does *not* lead to positive action, it becomes destructive—a negative force that you must stop feeding.

I once had a worry habit that had a major impact on my quality of life. I had mastered the art of embellishing my concerns, feeding my negative thoughts, and projecting them far beyond what was likely to happen. I found that the key to changing was to notice and break the thought pattern before it got too far. I learned to recognize when my worry was becoming a drama, when it was consuming too much of my thinking, and when my spirits dropped for more than a brief time. Taking appropriate action when I could—usually by giving myself a gentle reminder like *Don't go there*—made a difference. Rather than feed my worries, I learned to starve them.

Worry isn't the only kind of negative thought that can turn into an evil wolf of the mind. Anger is another emotion many people are inclined to feed. When we are angry, we also often feel righteous. *What happened to me just isn't fair,* we tell ourselves (and anyone else who appears sympathetic). *This isn't personal. It's about justice.* Of course, the fact that it *is* personal is demonstrated by the reality that people rarely get equally worked up about injustices that others suffer—only about injuries they themselves have felt.

Sometimes you may in fact have been treated unfairly. Maybe you were passed over for a promotion you deserved; maybe you were promised a raise that never materialized; maybe you were snubbed by a onetime friend, or treated with mockery or contempt by a relative. Under those circumstances resentment and anger may be understandable. You find yourself arguing your case in your mind like a lawyer making a presentation to a jury. And like the lawyer, you emphasize every fact and circumstance that supports your argument while ignoring or minimizing those that weaken it. The more you think about the injustice, the more one-sided the case you build and the more blind you become to other possibilities or explanations. As the bonfire grows, the more wood you pile on it to feed the flames. In a perverse way, the process is emotionally satisfying.

Yet dwelling on your anger, even when it is justifiable, rarely benefits you. In fact it's more likely to consume you. You become more and more obsessed with the resentment you feel and often end up doing and saying things you'll later regret.

Thankfully, there is an alternative. When you get irritated, bothered, or mad at someone, you can refuse to dwell on it and instead make an effort to forgive quickly and let it go.

This isn't always easy to do. Pride, self-interest, insecurity, and sensitivity can exacerbate your pain and make it harder to forgive. But curiosity—the brake on your Mood Elevator—can help. Rather than assume that the injustice you suffered was inexplicable and inexcusable, try looking for an explanation of what happened. Ask yourself, *What motivated this person to behave in such an unfair way? What thoughts, assumptions, beliefs, or emotions led them to think that this was an appropriate action to take?* Maybe the boss who passed you over for a promotion didn't realize how much you've contributed to the organization in the past year—or perhaps she was under pressure from her own boss to select a different candidate for the job. Maybe the friend who snubbed you was himself brooding over something you said that was unintentionally hurtful—or maybe he was depressed or distracted due to problems you know nothing about.

The people around us are usually motivated by forces very much like those that drive our own behavior. The difference lies in their perspective, which differs from our own. The more fully we understand that others are just doing what makes sense to them based on their thinking—flawed

as it may seem—the easier it is to depersonalize the irritation we feel and let it go.

You need to starve—not feed—the flames of anger. The
fuel is your escalating thoughts. The sooner you can break
the spell you seem to be under when anger consumes you,
the better off you (and those around you) will be.

The same goes for other negative feelings you may
be tempted to feed: impatience, defensiveness, insecurity,
self-righteousness, and the tendency to judge or blame.
When moods like these linger, force yourself to interrupt the pattern. Walk away from the conflict and take a
break from your self-justifying thoughts; engage in physical
exercise or spend time with a friend who is higher on the
Mood Elevator.

Escaping the Cycle of Depression

Depression is a longer-term visit to lower-level thinking,
driven by an ongoing story we invent and nurture. In many
people depression is fueled by a chemical imbalance that
can and should be treated medically. If you suspect that
you may be suffering from clinical depression, you owe it
to yourself and those you love to seek advice from a trained
professional who can help you manage the mental and
physical aspects of the condition.

In other cases, however, what people call "depression"
is simply a thought habit they get into, often for understandable reasons. The habit may be triggered initially by sad,

stressful, or painful circumstances—a death in the family, a major financial setback, a traumatic breakup. But in the end it is our thoughts and what we make of them that maintain the persistent low mood.

I had one period in my life, almost 40 years ago, when I faced a depression of this kind. My first wife was the first girl I loved—the Sunday school sweetheart of my boyhood. We dated through college and then married. I thought our marriage would last forever. When she left me, I became dysfunctional for a time. I fueled my sense of despair by dwelling on the pain of my loss, my apparent failure as a husband, and the death of my dreams for life.

Faith and hope got me to gradually shift my thinking. The turning point came when a wise and trusted friend sat me down and gave me a different set of thoughts on which to focus. He told me that while I couldn't see it now, I had a bright future. I was a likeable, desirable person, and someday I would love and be loved again. I had three little boys who loved me, and I could build whatever relationships I wanted with them. These and other elements of my future were in my hands.

As I reflected on my friend's words, I found my projections of the life before me becoming more optimistic. Rather than feed my sense of despair, I began having more hopeful thoughts of about my future possibilities. I formed a deep bond with my sons that persists to this day. And eventually I met and fell in love with Bernadette, with whom I built a richer, more fulfilling life.

The shift from despair to hope occurred by way of a change in my thinking and state of mind. Making a change like this is often slow and difficult, but it is certainly possible. If you find yourself suffering from a similar problem with depression, look for an opportunity to change your thinking. It may come in the form of a conversation with a friend, as in my case; it could occur through a religious or spiritual experience, time spent with family members, a change in your work or life surroundings, or some other unpredictable circumstance. Professional counseling may help. No matter how it happens, when you sense the possibility of changing your mind-set, try to embrace it. It may be the *up* button on the Mood Elevator that you've been seeking.

Choose the Moods You Will Feed

Look at the bottom half of the Mood Elevator. Which of those levels are most familiar to you? On which floors do you habitually linger? In what ways do you get caught up in feeding the emotions that nurture those moods? Consider the following questions:

▶ Are there certain things or people that make you impatient or frustrated? If so, do you find yourself brooding about those experiences, savoring the details and stoking the flames of your annoyance?

▶ Do you frequently feel irritated or bothered? If so, do you feed those emotions by complaining about them to friends and family or thinking about them continually?

▶ Do you have a worry habit? If so, do you tend to dramatize the negative things you fear, exaggerating their seriousness and ignoring the practical, concrete steps you can take to reduce their danger and minimize their effect?

▶ Are you habitually defensive or insecure? If so, do you feed those emotions by constantly reminding yourself of your weaknesses, failings, and mistakes while forgetting about your strengths, victories, and accomplishments?

▶ Are there people or things about which you tend to be judgmental and blaming? If so, do you overlook the pressures and problems others experience that may make it hard for them to resist temptation? Do you find yourself "keeping score" of all the bad things they've done (while perhaps ignoring or downplaying the equally questionable things you've done)?

Now look at the top half of the Mood Elevator. Which of these upper levels would you like to spend more time visiting? What steps can you take to feed the emotions that will open the doors to those moods? Here are some examples:

▶ Would you like to be more creative and innovative? If so, try giving yourself permission to expand your thinking to embrace more nonroutine, out-of-the-box concepts, whether on the job or in your personal life. Set aside time to brainstorm, daydream, and play with ideas. When some of the ideas you come up with seem to have potential, try sharing them with others.

▶ Would you like to be more hopeful and optimistic? If so, make time every day to think about your future in a positive, upbeat way. Imagine something you'd like to achieve, whether grand (finding a great new job) or modest (cleaning out your closet). Then take one concrete step toward making it happen.

▶ Would you like to be more appreciative? If so, set aside time to think about the good things in your life and the people or things that make them possible. Then express your gratitude—directly if possible (for example, saying thank you to your spouse, a colleague, or a friend) or symbolically if not (for example, offering prayers to the divinity of your choosing, or silently thanking an ancestor for the ways he or she enriched your life).

▶ Would you like to be more patient and understanding? If so, strengthen these traits by practicing them whenever they are needed. When stuck in line at the bank, use the time for a quiet moment of mini-meditation; when annoyed by a colleague's careless errors, offer to demonstrate a better way to get the job done.

▶ Would you like to be more flexible and adaptive? Feed those emotions by doing one new thing every day—or by doing one familiar thing in a new way. It might be as simple as trying a new route from your home to your work or as ambitious as helping launch a new community service organization in your town.

You don't have to be a passive passenger on your Mood Elevator, drifting from floor to floor unable to control or influence the journey. Make a conscious decision about where you want to spend your time and take steps to feed the emotions that will take you there.

Remember what the wise grandfather said: the one you feed is the one that wins.

Living in Mild Preference

What if the trials of this life are Your mercies in disguise?

—Laura Story

One of the lower levels on the Mood Elevator that many people drop into quite easily is the one labeled *irritated/ bothered*. When we find ourselves on this floor, we usually blame it on events, circumstances, or the people around us:

"Traffic was heavier than ever this morning."

"My spouse has a habit that irritates me."

"I don't get the appreciation I deserve at work."

"I have to spend half of my day at the office fixing the messes my colleague made."

"My cable service is down for the second time this month."

Of course, we all know that life can never be counted on to work out exactly as we hoped. What is interesting is that, given the same circumstances, some people become irritated and bothered very quickly, while others shrug it off and let it go. Some people seem to get off the Mood Elevator and remain on the irritated level for hours or even days; others just visit that floor occasionally, then quickly move on to different, higher levels.

A best-selling book by Richard Carlson addresses this topic—*Don't Sweat the Small Stuff and It's All Small Stuff: Simple Ways to Keep the Little Things from Taking Over Your Life.* Its popularity reflects the fact that this is a very common life condition.

What differentiates people who "don't sweat the small stuff" from people who seem to be irritated and bothered—even angry—practically every day? Those who are more easily upset by circumstances have a stronger need for things to go their way—and that way follows a single, preferred, clearly defined path. They have deep-seated beliefs about how people are supposed to behave, are locked into "principles" as they define them, and are less willing to compromise.

You might consider this an admirable trait. Isn't setting and insisting on high standards a worthy approach to life? No, because such devotion to self-proclaimed principles can easily evolve into rigidity. When you apply this philosophy, consciously or unconsciously, to small matters as well as to important ones, you are likely to spend a lot of time at the *irritated/bothered* level on the Mood Elevator. You'll end up hurting your relationships and making yourself unhappy unnecessarily—without actually improving the quality of your life circumstances.

Caring a Little about the Little Things in Life

People who spend less time in the lower-level moods adopt an attitude I call *mild preference.* Like everyone, they have their likes and dislikes. If they could have their way, every day would be a perfect one, marked by blue skies, a trouble-free workday, a blissful family life, and nothing but their favorite shows on TV. But they understand that life in the real world isn't like that. And when circumstances don't fit their desires or expectations, they do not respond with excessive or prolonged irritation; instead they allow their negative emotions to pass by like clouds in an otherwise sunny sky and then focus their energies in other, more positive directions.

Today's traffic is unusually congested? *Too bad, but I can use the extra time in the car to think about my presentation at this afternoon's meeting. Maybe I can come up with a better anecdote to illustrate my key concept.*

Did my spouse correct one of my exaggerated stories in public at last night's party—despite the fact that I've mentioned how much I dislike that? *Ouch! I wish she wasn't so honest sometimes. But I guess on any list of the worst habits a spouse could have—excessive drinking, dishonesty, physical or mental abuse—being more accurate than me is pretty far down the list.*

Wouldn't it be nice if I didn't have to get on planes and stay in hotels most weeks? *But that's a small price to pay to get to do work I love that makes a difference in the world. And the added benefit is that my relationship is always fresh, as we value our time together so much.*

Living in mild preference doesn't mean adopting a Pollyanna attitude: *Not a single problem! Everything's great.* It does mean looking for positive steps you can take to solve problems when they arise—and refusing to wallow in the emotions of frustration and anger that problems can so easily generate.

Living in mild preference does not mean having no standards or principles. It does mean being selective about how and when to apply your standards and principles—choosing your battles carefully, as the saying goes.

There may be a few critical issues in your life that are truly nonnegotiable. Matters that get to the heart of your identity, your vital self-interests, or the moral values you live by fall into this category. If a friend or loved one wants you to do something that could endanger you or that you would find ethically repugnant, you owe it to yourself to say no. If someone at work is cutting corners on product quality or customer service or is behaving in ways that violate the company's code of ethics, you may need to draw a line in the sand. But relatively few of life's daily issues merit this level of importance.

On close examination most of our everyday concerns qualify as "small stuff" to which mild preference should apply. Developing this sense of perspective and learning to apply it throughout your day is one of the fine arts of successful living.

Should we have Mexican or Italian for dinner? You probably prefer one or the other, but a disagreement about it need not turn into World War III. Which of these cover designs will look best on our company's new brochure? You may strongly prefer design A—but if your teammates choose design B, it's not a matter of life or death, and it doesn't mean that you work with "a bunch of idiots who couldn't care less about my input."

Bernadette and I have a remarkably peaceful and loving relationship. Living in mild preference goes a long way to help make that tranquility possible. It saves us from the kind of bickering that sours so many marriages—fights over where to go on vacation, what movie to watch, which friends to invite to dinner, and whom we are rooting for in politics. Sure, those things matter a little, but compared with maintaining our loving family, they're all small stuff.

Humor as a Tool for Combatting Rigidity

You've probably noticed that *sense of humor* is in the top half of the Mood Elevator map. Mild preference and an appreciation for the funny side of life are deeply connected. We are less apt to be fixed, rigid, and demanding in our preferences and needs when we can see the humor in our circumstances.

Air travel is a modern miracle that enables us to journey all over the globe at a fraction of the cost and time once required. Yet practically everyone has experienced how stressful, frustrating, and irritating travel can be. Perhaps that is why the most successful airline in US history uses humor as a key business strategy.

Southwest Airlines is a no-frills, no-first-class carrier that frequently earns top ratings for the quality of the customer experience. Their secret? Southwest hires people who are lighthearted and enjoy amusing others. When a flight is dogged by bad weather or mechanical problems, they keep people's spirits up by finding ways to turn the setback into a comedy rather than a tragedy.

Stories about the use of humor by Southwest people often circulate for years afterward. In the wake of one especially bumpy landing, a Southwest flight attendant took to the intercom to announce, "That was quite a bump, and I'm here to tell you it wasn't the airline's fault, it wasn't the pilot's fault, it wasn't the flight attendants' fault—it was the asphalt!"

On another flight, after an hour's delay on the runway, the captain apologized for the late start, then promised, "Don't worry, folks, we're going to fly this thing like we stole it!"

And in the wake of a much longer weather-related delay—on a plane with a number of impatient, irritated passengers—the flight attendant interrupted the routine safety announcement to comment, "For those of you traveling with small children, how is that working out for you?!"

I wouldn't go so far as to say that Southwest passengers *hope* for problems so that they can collect another great humor anecdote, but they do appreciate the fact that Southwest employees are experts at using a lighthearted attitude to lubricate the small annoyances in life. And this is a deliberate corporate strategy. When talking about the kind of people they look to hire, Southwest's co-founder, Herb Kelleher, said, "Life is too short and too hard and too serious not to be humorous about it. We look for attitudes, people with a sense of humor, who don't take themselves too seriously."[7]

Staying up the Mood Elevator enhances Southwest's success and profitability in two ways: by attracting more loyal customers and by making it easier for employees to operate at their best. The teamwork and camaraderie among Southwest employees helps them service, load, and unload airplanes faster than anyone else in the industry, which helps maintain the airline's exceptional on-time performance rate.

Everyone can learn from the Southwest Airlines example. When you're having a crazy day and encountering challenge upon challenge, you can become grim *or* you can take a deep breath, put the problems in perspective, and look for the humor in the insanity that surrounds you. If you can learn to laugh at the occasional absurdities of life, it will raise your spirits and enable you to access your full wisdom. As a result, you can tackle the day's problems in a healthier and more productive way.

Take Your Thinking More Lightly

During down times it is easy to become trapped in lower-level thinking—and down times are when your thinking is most unreliable. Paradoxically, we tend to take our faulty thinking most seriously just when we should discount it the most. Learning to take your thinking more lightly—to question your own assumptions, to doubt your own certainty, and to be open to opposing ideas and contrary evidence, especially when your low mood is talking—can dramatically improve your quality of life.

Lots of benefits come from cultivating the habit of taking your thinking more lightly:

▶ You will be a better listener.

▶ You will perceive your surroundings more accurately.

▶ You will be more open to new ideas.

▶ You will recall critical information in a timely fashion.

▶ You will see a broader range of possibilities and solutions.

▶ You will respond to challenges more creatively.

▶ You will feel more optimistic and hopeful.

▶ You will remain higher up the Mood Elevator.

Letting go of lower-state thoughts and feelings is not always easy or possible.

Here is a way to use your feelings as a guide. When a down-side emotion like impatience, irritation, anxiety, or judgment surfaces in you, don't react immediately. First pause and simply *notice* the feeling so that you can choose how to respond to it rather than react on autopilot. Next, *make a conscious decision* as to whether the situation is significant enough to react strongly to or whether it is "small stuff" for which an attitude of mild preference is more appropriate.

In most cases, you'll want to choose to live in mild preference. But if you do decide that a particular circumstance warrants a more emphatic response, you will do so in a much more thoughtful, effective way because you paused to make a conscious choice rather than react automatically.

Here's a metaphor I use to remind myself of the benefits of mild preference and taking my thinking lightly: Like many air travelers, I prefer to avoid waiting for checked luggage by using a carry-on bag equipped with wheels that let me roll it down the airplane aisle. In most cases, this works like a charm. But some airplanes have narrower aisles than others, and the difference of an inch or two sometimes causes my bag to bang into the seats on either side of the aircraft, annoying my fellow passengers and making my trip down the aisle more difficult. And the problem is much worse when I am anxious or in a hurry. The faster I try to go, the more the bag bounces off one armrest and rams into the other. Sometimes my bag even flips over sideways, and I end up dragging it down the aisle. Those few inches of aisle width make all the difference.

Life is like that. When you live with strong preferences, unyielding principles, and rigid thinking, it's like trying to navigate down a narrow aisle—you keep bumping into thought patterns and feelings you could easily avoid. Instead, try broadening your aisle just a bit by making a deliberate choice to be more flexible, open-minded, and lighthearted. You'll find yourself feeling irritated, bothered, and judgmental a lot less often—and enjoying life a lot more.

Shifting Your Set Point: The Wellness Equation

The greatest discovery of my generation is that a human being can alter his life by altering his attitudes of mind.

—WILLIAM JAMES

The benefits of living life up the Mood Elevator are obvious. Fortunately, most people seem to be born with access to a naturally healthy state of mind. Our default setting is to be up the Mood Elevator. That's our home base—and it's only a thought away.

Medical experts tells us that all people have a "set point" when it comes to body temperature—a personal temperature index that is close to the normal 98.6 degrees Fahrenheit but that may be slightly higher or slightly lower. Similarly, most people have a set point for their weight—the number we fluctuate around and keep coming back to.

We also tend to have a set point on the Mood Elevator—one that we can shift through a couple of deliberate life practices. One practice involves adjusting your habitual mental state through certain simple behavior adjustments. I discuss this practice in chapter 10.

The other practice is simply taking better care of ourselves physically—something we all know we are supposed to do but that we often neglect through carelessness or being overly busy.

Research shows that when people are run-down they catch colds more easily. We also catch bad moods more easily. When we are physically run-down, we are more sensitive to what other people say and more likely to take things personally. We are less patient and understanding and often feel overwhelmed. Because the quality of our thinking is lower when we are tired, we are not as wise and resourceful as we could be. Our effectiveness is hampered, and that increases the stress and pressure we feel. We handle life better when we are fit and rested.

By contrast, when we are rested and in good physical shape, we are more resilient, less easily irritated or bothered, and less prone to having our buttons pushed by people or circumstances. That's because there is a strong connection between our physical state and our mental state, and that is why, for most people, life looks better after a good night's sleep, a restful weekend, or a refreshing vacation.

Fortunately, there are specific ways to take better care of yourself so that you will be more resilient and less apt to drift down to the lower floors on the Mood Elevator.

The Importance of the Stretch-and-Recover Cycle

The foundation of best practices for physical fitness is an understanding of the need of both your body and your mind to stretch and recover. Humans were designed to live in cycles. To operate at our best, we need cycles of stretch and recovery in many aspects of our lives.

Experienced athletes generally know how the stretch-and-recover cycle works. Stretching means going beyond your comfort zone to expand your capabilities mentally, emotionally, and physically. Weight lifters, for example, work one part of the body very hard to break down their muscles; they then let that body part rest the next day so that it recovers, grows, and becomes stronger.

Tennis players alternate great bursts of energy with brief recovery times. Many have recovery rituals, such as playing with their racket strings or bouncing the ball between vigorous sets.

Having been a jogger for decades, several years ago I decided to take up triathlons. The cross-training involved in preparing for a triathlon yields a natural stretch-and-recover cycle. When I run one day and bike or swim the next, I use varying muscle groups, giving other muscle groups the chance to rest and recover.

The concept of stretch-and-recover is relevant in mental fitness, as well. The upper floors on the Mood Elevator—like those labeled *curious/interested, flexible/adaptive, hopeful/optimistic, resourceful,* and *creative/innovative*—all involve activities that help us stretch: learning new things, tackling challenging assignments, and taking calculated risks, professionally and personally. Research shows that these activities expand our minds, adding brain cells and warding off mental decline in later years. Rest through meditation also has an impact on brain function.

But we can stretch for only so long before burning out, so we also need ways to recover mentally. Processes that encourage mental recovery include sleep, exercise, and time spent in certain self-renewing, higher mood states such as those labeled *grateful, appreciative, patient/understanding,* and *sense of humor.*

Getting Enough Sleep

The most important recovery mechanism people have is simply getting enough sleep. American author and entrepreneur E. Joseph Cossman allegedly said, "The best bridge between despair and hope is a good night's sleep." When we're well rested, we feel stronger and more capable, and we have better access to our wisest self. That's why the natural alternation of day and night and the instinctive circadian cycle of activity and sleep has shaped human society for thousands of years. And yet in our nonstop, 24/7, Internet-driven world, the majority of people are sleep deprived.

Being sleep deprived isn't just unpleasant; it has been associated with numerous medical problems, including obesity, diabetes, high blood pressure, stroke, and cardiovascular disease. Sleep deprivation is also closely associated with such psychiatric disorders as alcoholism and bipolar disorder. In fact, up to 90 percent of adults suffering from depression are found to have sleep difficulties.[8]

Adequate sleep is also important for learning, gaining insights, and making decisions.

People who lack sufficient sleep perform less well in solving problems, completing puzzles, and taking tests. Research has shown that sleep-deprived subjects score lower on tests of both IQ (intelligence) and EQ (emotional intelligence). They have less access to creative original thought, and their ability to handle stressful situations and deal with people suffers.[9]

Scientists have yet to determine all the ways that sleep benefits us, but research provides some clues. Sleep provides time for the body and mind to recover. When the brain slows down, especially during deep, non–rapid eye movement (NREM) sleep, it shifts from generating alpha waves to delta waves, which are therapeutic and restful. When denied NREM sleep for too long, experimental subjects became near-psychotic, experiencing hallucinations and paranoid schizophrenic thoughts.[10]

Rapid eye movement (REM) sleep plays a different but equally important role. According to Rebecca Spencer, professor of psychology at the University of Massachusetts, REM sleep activates the emotional areas of the brain so that "the things that are most important to you on a gut level are prioritized." It also appears that, during REM sleep, all the conscious and unconscious images we perceived during the day are processed and organized. As Spencer puts it, "REM sleep is good for problem-solving and decision-making because your brain is putting pieces together and trying new alternatives. You gain insights that wouldn't occur to you when you were awake."[11]

This may explain the common observation that "sleeping on a problem" often helps generate a solution. In one study experimental subjects played a game with a hidden underlying rule: one group of subjects had a chance to sleep before discussing the game the next morning, while another group played the game in the morning and debriefed it later that day. Among those who "slept on it," twice as many participants figured out the secret rule.[12]

Senn Delaney has found something similar in its culture-shaping sessions with executive teams: while a one-day session can provide value, a two-day session that includes reflection and discussion the second morning is usually much more transformational.

If you are among the millions of people who are habitually sleep deprived, make changing your sleep habits a high priority. Stop settling for five or six hours a night; reorganize your schedule so that you can routinely enjoy seven or eight hours of sleep. If necessary, alter your sleeping conditions to be more conducive to relaxation and rest: get room-darkening curtains, remove the television or computer, install sound-proofing insulation, and set a comfortable temperature.

You'll accomplish far more in 16 hours after a good night's sleep than you can in 18 or 19 hours after a too-short period of rest and recovery.

The Power of Exercise: The "Use It or Lose It" Principle

Exercise is a vital component of any plan to live a healthier and longer life. My interest in running developed decades ago when I read Dr. Kenneth Cooper's original book, titled simply *Aerobics*. Cooper was the first to popularize the notion that there is a connection between aerobic exercise and cardiovascular health. Prior to that, bed rest and a sedentary life was the common prescription for those with heart problems. Cooper's motto was *Use it or lose it*, and hundreds of studies have documented the validity of that premise. The body doesn't wear out; it rusts out from lack of use.

I was in pretty good shape when I was young. I was a basketball player in high school, a gymnast in college, and a recreational league basketball player into my late twenties. Then I got busy launching a consulting business and raising three kids, and I stopped exercising much. As a result, I packed on 35 pounds.

Aerobics was my wake-up call. It contained a self-administered fitness test designed by Cooper for use with the military. The test was simple: Run as far as you can in 12 minutes, with the outcome evaluated according to your age and gender. I made it a couple of blocks before I was gasping for air with an ache in my side. I knew I was out of shape and in trouble. I started running regularly.

That was almost 50 years ago and, like the movie character Forrest Gump, I haven't stopped running since. To save my knees, several years ago I began cross-training with road biking and swimming. The weight came off and stayed off, thanks to the combination of regular exercise and a healthy diet.

The Cooper Clinic in Dallas continues to do great research on the connection between exercise and heart disease. Researchers there have proven that even those who exercise moderately have measurably less chance of heart problems than do sedentary people.

Aerobic exercise has other powerful benefits. Studies by psychology professor Arthur F. Kramer of the University of Illinois at Urbana-Champaign found that simple aerobic exercise (such as vigorous walking for 45 minutes three times a week) improved memory by 20 percent. Even more dramatic, a year of intense exercise can give a 70-year-old the mental functioning of a 30-year-old: improved memory, enhanced planning skills, and an increased ability to deal with ambiguity and handle simultaneous tasks. As Kramer says, "You can think of fitness training as changing the molecular and cellular building blocks that underlie many cognitive skills."[13]

If you are suffering from physical, mental, and emotional weariness—and spending too many days among the bottom floors on your Mood Elevator—try incorporating aerobic exercise into your daily routine. You may be startled by the positive results you'll experience.

Aerobics and Beyond

There are three forms of exercise that make sense to me. Of these the first and most important is *aerobic exercise,* which gets the heart rate up and provides all the benefits just described.

The second is *anaerobic exercise,* otherwise known as resistance or strength training. It too contributes to vitality and stamina.

Strengthening your muscles, especially core muscles like those in and around your abdomen, back, and pelvis, contributes enormously to a more satisfying life. Exercising your abs not only keeps your stomach from expanding with age but also protects your back, reducing the aches and pains that can take you down the Mood Elevator.

Resistance training also increases your metabolism and contributes to weight loss or weight maintenance as you age. Because it builds bone density, it enables you to engage in more-vigorous activities without significant physical limitations. Resistance training also appears to have definite psychological benefits. A 2001 study published in the *Archives of Internal Medicine* found that just one or two resistance sessions per week for one year improved mental acuity and cognitive performance.[14]

The third and perhaps most neglected form of exercise is *stretching.* Our joints and tendons contract as we age, and we become less flexible, so we need to apply the stretch-and-recover model to our joints and tendons too.

I stretch regularly, motivated by an image in my mind of what could happen if I stopped. When shopping at a mall near my home, I sometimes see elderly people from a local retirement community trying to back their cars out of parking places. Their biggest challenge? They can't turn their necks far enough to see what's behind them. That painful prospect provides an incentive to me to stretch my neck, back, and hamstrings regularly. My friends who have taken up yoga tell me it's a wonderful way to give their bodies the stretching they need while also providing a dose of mental and spiritual refreshment.

To Reap the Benefits of Exercise, Start Small—But Start Now

In addition to extending your life span and reducing your susceptibility to disease, exercise plays a major role in mental fitness and in raising your set point on the Mood Elevator.

There are many physiological reasons for this. Exercise increases your blood flow and builds your stamina, so you don't tire as easily. It also produces endorphins—a category of chemicals that act like a safe, legal narcotic to give you a positive, high-energy feeling. In fact, a meta-analysis of more than 100 studies on the impact of exercise published in the *American Journal of Psychiatry* concluded, "Exercise improves mental health and well-being, reduces stress and anxiety and enhances cognitive functioning."[15]

I have found this to be true in my own life. If I can get in even a brief run early in the morning before work, it raises my spirits and helps me start my day with a clearer mind and a fresher point of view. Many of the ideas in this book came to me while I was jogging. I'm not sure where these exercise-driven insights come from, but they are almost always more inspiring and interesting than the thoughts I have while working at my computer.

Yes, fitting an exercise regimen into your busy work-week can be challenging—but don't let that be an excuse to do nothing. In the short term, make a commitment to at least a modest program of physical fitness. Promise yourself that you'll get a good night's sleep, take a 10-minute walk during a break at work, and build a stretch break into at least one meeting over the course of your day.

All of these small steps will elevate your spirit. In time, as the benefits slowly begin to mount, you'll probably find yourself wanting to carve out more time for a more ambitious exercise program—and your time on the Mood Elevator's upper floors will steadily increase as a result.

The Foods You Choose

Hundreds of books have been written on diet and nutrition. I don't have the scientific expertise or the desire to compete with them here. But make no mistake—there is a direct link between what you eat and the quality of your travels on the Mood Elevator.

The biggest problem with the typical American diet is that it is overprocessed and high in salt, fat, and sugar, which puts on weight and damages the cardiovascular system, leading to heart disease, stroke, erectile dysfunction, and other ailments that slow us down, reduce our quality of life, and lead to early death. And these problems aren't confined to a small fraction of Americans: nearly one-third of the US population falls into the obese category, and nearly 60 percent of Americans are overweight.

While diets work for a few, most diets don't work over the long term. My experience suggests that the best way of eating right for health and weight is to find healthful foods you can eat as a permanent lifestyle—not as a short-term diet.

My own journey toward healthy eating habits started around the time I failed Dr. Cooper's aerobics test. I had a regular checkup with my family doctor, which included a blood test. My physician casually mentioned that my cholesterol was a little high and suggested, "You might want to switch from whole milk to low fat." This was back in the 1970s, and I hadn't heard much about the link between cholesterol and heart disease. I looked up all the references I could find and began to educate myself.

I learned that saturated fats in particular contribute to blocked arteries. The case was best stated by Jon N. Leonard, Jack L. Hofer, and Nathan Pritikin in *Live Longer Now: The First One Hundred Years of Your Life*. Neither a medical doctor nor a nutritionist, Pritikin was an engineer who became interested in health matters when he found out that he suffered from heart disease. He discovered that countries where people consume the most fat had the most arterial disease. Over time he created a program that was a revolutionary departure from current medical thinking and tested it on friends and relatives.

In 1974 he opened the Pritikin Longevity Center in Santa Barbara, California. Its success against illnesses such as heart disease, diabetes, arthritis, and gout proved greater than even Pritikin had dreamed. Eighty-five percent of those who came to the center on medication for high blood pressure left with normal blood pressure and no medication. Half of those with adult-onset diabetes left insulin-free, and more than half of those who were already scheduled for heart bypass surgery left the center no longer needing the operation.

The diet plan Pritikin devised was high in whole grains, vegetables, and dietary fiber, while deriving less than 10 percent of total calories from fats. Today this basic formula has been incorporated into the guidelines on how to reduce the risk of developing cardiovascular disease by such mainstream organizations as the American Heart Association.

My study of Pritikin's work prompted me to reduce the fats in my diet and increase the vegetables, fruits, and high-fiber whole grains. I later learned that saturated fats (like those found in animal products) are bad for you, while unsaturated fats (like the omega-3 oils found in olive oil and fatty fish like salmon) are good for you. I also learned about the power of antioxidants found in certain berries.

Studies continue to link diet to disease. The strongest link appears to be to animal products—red meats in particular. In a 2010 report by researchers at the Harvard School of Public Health, data from more than 400,000 people over a 10-year period showed that just a 2-ounce daily serving of processed meat (like hot dogs, bacon, or lunch meat) increased the risk of diabetes by 50 percent, while just 4 ounces of unprocessed red meat (such as hamburger or steak) increased diabetes risk by 20 percent.[16]

Similarly, a National Institutes of Health and AARP study found that men who ate the most red meat had a 31 percent higher overall death rate that those who ate the least.[17] Other studies have documented the health problems caused by the excessive sugar in soft drinks and the refined flour in most of the baked goods we eat. The rise in diabetes has a direct correlation to the increased use of sweeteners like high-fructose corn syrup and the rise of obesity.

All this information led me to create some simple guidelines that I follow for energy, longevity, and weight control. I try to avoid or limit fats and sugars:

▶ Saturated fats from dairy products, processed or red meat, and the wrong oils (saturated or trans fats) found in most processed food

▶ Simple carbohydrates and non–naturally occurring sugars found in pastries, desserts, soft drinks, white flour, and most fruit juices

On the other hand, these are what I try to get plenty of:

► Vegetables, whole fruits, and nuts like almonds and walnuts

► Protein mainly from legumes (beans and lentils) and other plant products like soy. If more protein is needed, I use plant-based protein powder supplements. For meat, I choose fish, such as wild-caught salmon or tuna.

► The right oils, especially those that have high levels of omega-3s

► Fiber from vegetables, as well as grains such as brown rice, oatmeal, and whole wheat

► Antioxidants, such as those found in blueberries, acai berries, and pomegranate juice

► Water, while limiting juice consumption and cutting out soft drinks

It took me quite a while to develop and implement these guidelines for myself. I have dropped some foods I loved and added healthy ones I can live with as an ongoing lifestyle choice. The key is developing increased consciousness about the right and wrong kinds of foods to eat. That leads to selecting more of the right kinds of foods and avoiding the damaging ones. In time the healthy foods become a preference and a way of life.

I do know that what I eat makes a difference. The cholesterol that my doctor told me was a bit high back in the

1970s—it was 220 then— was more recently measured at 150. I have very low LDL (low-density lipoprotein, or "bad" cholesterol) and triglycerides and very high HDL (high-density lipoprotein, or "good" cholesterol), as well as other favorable blood markers. I entered my first sprint triathlon around 10 years ago at age 70. I now participate in about six triathlons per year, most often as the only competitor in the 80-and-above age category.

I believe this is possible because of my healthy diet and my commitment to regular exercise. The combination also contributes to a lot more time up the Mood Elevator. I hope you'll try embarking on your own journey of well-being. You'll be glad you did.

Quieting Your Mind

Quiet the mind and the soul will speak.

—MA JAYA SATI BHAGAVATI

In chapter 9 we looked at the importance of the stretch-and-recover cycle as a basic principle of physical fitness that also applies to mental, emotional, and spiritual fitness. Developing the ability to move from a very busy mind to a quiet mind is central to living up the Mood Elevator. The nature of thought on the lower levels, like worry or anger, is frenetic and circular. In the highest state on the elevator—*grateful*—there is almost no thought, just a good calm feeling. This quieter state allows both mind and body to rest and recover from the strain of everyday life.

That has become increasingly difficult in our digital, broadband-driven world. We are constantly bombarded with information, demanding our attention and scattering our focus. I met a CEO recently who said that when he sends a text message or email to someone on his senior team, he expects a response within 30 minutes—a rule that applies

24 hours a day, seven days a week. While this is an extreme case, more and more people do feel the need to respond to work-related messages no matter when they arrive. As a result, evenings, weekends, holidays, and vacations are no longer times for mental refreshment, recreation, and relaxation. They are often periods of stress and anxiety that simply extend the workweek rather than enable you to recover from it.

Making Time to "Be Here Now"

Higher-quality thinking *feels* different from lower-quality thinking. In the higher mood states, our thoughts are quieter, more flowing, clearer, and relaxed. Feelings like gratitude, love, serenity, and peace come with almost no effort. Spending time with those feelings, in what you might call *being states,* provides precious recovery time that greatly enhances our emotional and psychological well-being.

Think about the last time you were in such a being state. Maybe it was a moment when you were overwhelmed by a beautiful scene in nature, delighted by the pure love of a child, transported by the grandeur of a piece of music, or moved by an act of generosity or forgiveness directed toward you. During such moments, your mind is quiet and your thoughts are still. Life feels like an undisturbed, flowing river. When we are completely focused on "being here now," the surface of our emotions is calm and transparent, even though lots of water may be flowing underneath.

By contrast, when you are down the Mood Elevator, your thinking is busy, cloudy, and unclear. You tend to get caught up in eddies of worry, anger, insecurity, judgment, and other emotions that swirl around and spiral downward. Learning to recognize and calm those mental eddies can help destress your life.

Two techniques help me achieve that quieter state of mind. One is to compartmentalize my work time and my off time.

Make no mistake, I live a busy, high-pressure life, just like most people today. That means I often take some work home at night, on weekends, and on vacation. There are times when I need to respond to urgent messages from the office or a client, even when I am officially "not at work."

I minimize the impact of these pressures on my psychological and spiritual state, however, by ensuring that I am *not* mentally at work all the time. I block off time for me to be here now with the people and activities I care about. I consciously cultivate my ability to be fully present in the moment with a quiet mind.

Of course, this is a challenge for me—as it probably is for you. Most of us get so caught up in our thinking that special moments in life pass us by. Have you ever had a day off when your working mind never shut down? Have you taken a vacation when only your body was present? Have you ever spent time with a loved one only to realize that your thoughts and concerns were far away? These are all examples of *not* being here now. They are also lost opportunities to refresh, renew, recover, and connect with people on a deeper level.

This is not a brand-new problem. Many philosophical and religious traditions teach that happiness is to be found by living in the present moment. And modern science has confirmed this ancient truth. In an article titled "A Wandering Mind Is an Unhappy Mind," psychologists Matthew Killingsworth and Daniel Gilbert describe their investigations into the relationship between a wandering mind and happiness in the real world. They developed a web application for the iPhone that allowed them to randomly sample the emotional status, activities, and mind states of about 5,000 people from 83 different countries. They found that most of their subjects spent at least half their time thinking about something other than their immediate surroundings—and that most of this thinking did not make them happy.[18]

Knowing that I am just as susceptible to this tendency as anyone else, I make a conscious effort to combat it. Practical steps to compartmentalize my attention are very helpful. I turn my smartphone off during my son's volleyball games, on most evenings, and during large blocks of my weekend and vacation time. When I am away from the office, I allocate brief blocks of time to catch up on emails, but then I shut down my electronic connections, as well as my thinking about work. This provides not only recovery time for me but also more quality time with my loved ones.

The Role of Breathing in Quieting Your Mind

The second technique I employ to find those peaceful, centering moments we all need is a quick, simple way to quiet my mind in the midst of a hectic day. I merely stop, take a deep breath, and as I exhale I say to myself, *Be here now.* This exercise somehow has a centering effect and clears my thoughts, at least for the moment. It works remarkably well when I'm walking from one meeting to another or before opening the door when I get home at night.

I am not the only person who has discovered the amazing impact of breathing on one's state of mind, of course. Research has shown that slow, deep breathing somehow triggers the parasympathetic nervous system, which induces calm.

I was first introduced to the power of breathing when I read *The Relaxation Response* by Herbert Benson of Harvard Medical School. Benson studied Eastern meditation techniques and found that merely repeating a particular word or phrase each time you exhale while in a relaxed position has the effect of quieting the mind. While a Buddhist practitioner or someone who follows Deepak Chopra would use a mantra like *so hum,* Benson found that repeating the neutral word "one" on the exhale produced a similar result. He documented through research that the same exercise reduces pulse rate and blood pressure.

I've proven this myself by being able to drop my resting pulse rate from its normal 60 beats per minute to as low as

46; and I can lower my blood pressure to 90/50, when it is usually 20 to 30 points higher. I have used my own form of Benson's relaxation response technique and variants of it for years to start most days from a quieter, more grateful place.

More recently, I was introduced to author and psychologist John Selby, who also points to the power of breathing—but with a twist. In *Quiet Your Mind,* Selby's theory is that if you give the mind two or more tasks to perform, it can't wander. The result is a quieter mind. In practice, he recommends breathing through the nose while noticing the air as it moves in and out. If that is not enough to quiet your mind, the second simultaneous task is to notice the rise and fall of your chest or stomach. The concentration required to do both of these things at once makes other, more complex thinking difficult, resulting in a quieter mind.

When I am in the midst of a busy day, I simply take a few deep breaths whenever I feel I am ramping up, becoming too intense, or getting caught up in distracting anxieties and worries. It's a useful shortcut that helps me achieve a quieter mind in just a few seconds. Try one or more of the techniques I've described and see whether they make a difference for you.

Cultivating Gratitude

To speak gratitude is courteous and pleasant,
to enact gratitude is generous and noble,
but to live gratitude is to touch Heaven.

—JOHANNES A. GAERTNER

I recently watched a YouTube video called "The Power of
Words"—one that more than 25 million other people had
also watched.[19] It shows a man sitting on a city sidewalk
with a tin can for donations and a sign reading, I'M BLIND
PLEASE HELP. Passersby come and go, but very few make
a donation.

Then a woman comes along. She looks at the man's
sign, thinks for a minute, then flips it over and writes a new
message on it.

Almost immediately, the donations dramatically
increase. The blind man is both confused and amazed to
hear the shower of coins landing at his feet and in his can.
When the woman returns later in the day, the man asks her,
"What did you do to my sign?"

She replies, "I wrote the same—but in different words."

Then the sign is revealed: IT'S A BEAUTIFUL DAY AND
I **CAN'T** SEE IT.

That little video evoked powerful emotions in me.
What was it about the new message that induced so many
passersby to give generously to the blind man? It was the
power of *gratitude*—a feeling that is always available to all
of us but that we too often neglect in the rush of everyday
life. Being reminded of the miracle of sight made the people
who saw the sign newly aware of how lucky they were—and
in their gratitude they opened their hearts and shared some
of their bounty with a man less fortunate than themselves.

Counting your blessings is more than a platitude; it is
a pretty good way to maintain perspective on the realities
of your life.

Choosing the Gratitude Perspective

I have often been asked why the word *grateful* appears at
the very top of the Mood Elevator map. There are several
reasons.

Gratitude is what we might call an *overriding emotion.*
It is almost impossible to be grateful and at the same time be
angry, depressed, irritated, or self-righteous. There is a sense
of calm, warmth, and happiness that comes with gratitude
that overrides impatience, frustration, and anger. Because
gratitude is an emotion that connects us to a higher spirit,
it helps us feel more purposeful, present, and supportive
of those around us. And because gratitude is focused more
on others than on ourselves, it lifts us above lower mood

states like envy and enables us to escape from feelings of powerlessness or of being victimized.

Above all, gratitude is about *perspective*—about appreciating the realities of life and all it has to offer.

Consider this: The fact that you are reading this book means you are devoting time to thinking about self-actualization—to maximizing your potential and abilities and to making your life as rich, rewarding, and meaningful as possible. By definition, that means you are *not* focused on where your next meal is coming from or on how you can put a roof over your head. In other words, you already have a lot going for you. You are among the privileged of humankind who are not living at a subsistence level but rather can take the bare necessities of life—food, clothing, and a place to live—more or less for granted. Millions of your fellow human beings aren't so lucky—and not just in developing countries but closer to home, as well.

If you've ever seen a homeless person pushing a shopping cart containing all of their possessions down the street; or a child in a developing nation trailing after a tourist, begging for a penny or two; or a refugee family from a war zone desperately pleading for permission to cross the border into a land at peace, you know how blessed you and I are, no matter what problems and challenges we may face on an average day.

Does that mean we automatically feel a sense of gratitude every morning when we wake up? Unfortunately, no. That's where perspective comes in.

If we choose to focus our thoughts on what we don't have or don't like, we won't feel good about life. We will quickly head down the Mood Elevator—and stay there. Most of the lower-level mood states represent times when we have lost perspective. And when we ignore the many *good* things in our lives, the things we don't like can become overwhelming and consume us.

By contrast, if we choose to fully appreciate all that we have, we can experience life as full, rich, and rewarding. At the very least, we can be grateful for the gift of life itself. Just to have consciousness and to experience the world around us is a treasure that we usually overlook—just as the passersby in the video did, until the revised sign reminded them of its value.

Like so much else in life, being and feeling grateful is a matter of choice. Choosing to adopt the gratitude perspective is a powerful way to overcome negativity in your life. Bringing to mind something, anything, that you are grateful for can snap you out of a bad mood—and lift you back up to higher emotional levels. Gratitude is your always available "express button" on the Mood Elevator.

The Benefits of Gratitude

Choosing the gratitude perspective can lift you from the bottom to the top on the Mood Elevator, but being grateful isn't just about feeling good. There's abundant evidence that cultivating gratitude as a habitual way of thinking about life can have powerful psychological and emotional benefits.

Stephen Post is a researcher and professor of bioethics at Case Western Reserve University School of Medicine in Cleveland. Post founded a research group dedicated to testing and measuring the effects of love and other positive, caring emotions. His studies have shown that love-related qualities like gratitude actually make us physically healthier in at least five different ways:

- ▶ **Gratitude defends.** Just 15 minutes a day spent focusing on the things you are grateful for will significantly increase your body's natural antibodies, enhancing your immunity to disease.

- ▶ **Gratitude sharpens.** People who adopt the gratitude perspective are more focused mentally and measurably less vulnerable to suffering from clinical depression.

- ▶ **Gratitude calms.** A grateful state of mind induces a physiological state called *resonance* that is associated with healthier blood pressure and heart rate.

- ▶ **Gratitude strengthens.** Caring for others (a parent or an ailing loved one) can be draining—but grateful caregivers are healthier, more robust, and more capable than less grateful ones.

- ▶ **Gratitude heals.** Recipients of donated organs who have the most grateful attitudes heal faster from their surgical procedures.[20]

Post isn't the only researcher to uncover evidence of the health-enhancing power of gratitude. Research by University of California, Davis, psychology professor Robert A. Emmons indicates that "grateful people take better care of themselves and engage in more protective health behaviors like regular exercise, a healthy diet, [and] regular physical examinations."[21] Emmons also finds that grateful people tend to be more optimistic, a characteristic that boosts the immune system.[22]

Another fascinating and illuminating research project titled "Dimensions and Perspectives of Gratitude," sponsored by the John Templeton Foundation and led by Emmons, found that people who kept gratitude journals received many benefits. They exercised more regularly, reported fewer physical symptoms, felt better about their lives overall, were more optimistic when facing life's challenges, and made better progress toward their work or life goals.[23]

Sonja Lyubomirsky, a professor of psychology at the University of California, Riverside, focused on the mechanisms underlying gratitude in her book *The How of Happiness: A New Approach to Getting the Life You Want.* She identified activities that help raise your set point for happiness:

▶ Expressing gratitude

▶ Cultivating optimism

- ▶ Avoiding social comparisons

- ▶ Performing acts of kindness

- ▶ Nurturing relationships

- ▶ Forgiving others

- ▶ Pursuing "flow" experiences

- ▶ Savoring life's pleasures

- ▶ Pursuing spiritual growth

- ▶ Exercising and other good health practices

Gregory L. Fricchione, MD, director of the Benson-Henry Institute for Mind Body Medicine at Massachusetts General Hospital, sums up these and other studies as constituting "a wave of research that is sweeping the field of psychology and demonstrating that positive feelings have downstream health-promoting effects." Links between gratitude and several of the most important mood-regulating organs of the brain help explain, in Dr. Fricchione's words, "why you feel better when you recognize and appreciate the good in your life."[24]

The bottom line: If you want to be happier, forget the myth that achievements or acquisitions will bring happiness. Instead focus on activities that will nourish your sense of gratitude and your appreciation for the blessings you've already been granted.

Learning to Access Gratitude

All the higher levels on the Mood Elevator tend to be accompanied by a quieter mind. Gratitude is no different. It is difficult, if not impossible, to access with a very busy mind. That's why the feeling of gratitude is often connected with prayer or meditation, both of which quiet the mind and open the door to a broader, richer perspective on life.

Learning to access gratitude is a very personal thing. Like learning to better ride the Mood Elevator, accessing gratitude needs to be self-taught through trial and error. It is like learning to ride a two-wheeled bicycle: someone can explain it to you, but you have to get the feel for it yourself.

Several practices contribute to an ongoing mind-set of gratitude:

- ► In her book *Thank You Power,* journalist Deborah Norville suggests writing in a journal as a way to record and reflect on what you are grateful for.

- ► In his book *Flourish,* Martin Seligman describes a simple exercise that he calls Three Blessings: once a day bring to mind three small things that lift your spirits. They can be as simple as a great meal, a hug from a loved one, or a soft pillow on which to fall asleep.

- ► I take the first few minutes when I wake up to quiet my mind using the breathing techniques discussed

in chapter 10. Then I spend a few minutes thinking about the things I appreciate in my life. I use
a similar routine at night before going to sleep.

▶ I try to remain alert and sensitive to happenings
throughout my day that can remind me to be grateful—for example, any expression of love from one
of my five children, whether in the form of a hug,
a handwritten note, or a text message.

▶ Family rituals can nurture your gratitude perspective. Many families take turns expressing gratitude
as part of their Thanksgiving dinner. Our family has
turned this into an everyday dinner ritual. After a
brief thank-you prayer for the meal, each person
at the table shares something they feel really good
about from that day. This ritual evokes a spirit of
gratitude and a warm connection between us.

▶ Our family also occasionally devotes a dinner to
"what I appreciate about you," in which we each
share one thing we appreciate about another
family member.

It has been said that humans pass along only one out
of every 30 good thoughts we have about others. Making a
habit of generously sharing our appreciation for the people
around us nurtures relationships and lifts the spirits of those
on both the giving and receiving ends.

Gratitude in the Face of Adversity

Contrary to what you might assume, gratitude is not just for people whose lives are filled with obvious blessings. Many people embrace a gratitude perspective in response to profound adversity—for example, by gaining a new appreciation for just being alive after a life-threatening event. In a way it's unfortunate that it takes a near-death experience or some other trauma to put the blessing of life in perspective. But when we are caught up in the challenges of everyday life, we easily lose sight of what's most important. Adversity can become a blessing in disguise when it encourages us to recover our awareness of the beauty and wonder of ordinary existence.

You probably know someone who has gained, or regained, their gratitude perspective in the wake of hard times. My sister-in-law Sybil has been much more light-hearted and grateful for the little things in life since her successful battle with breast cancer. Compared with what she went through then, everything else is "small stuff."

The gratitude perspective can be one of our most powerful tools for dealing with adversity in life. As we've already seen, living among the top floors on the Mood Elevator helps you operate at your best, making it easier to find creative solutions to the toughest challenges.

I needed to be at my best when I faced three simultaneous major life challenges in the year 2000.

At the end of the dot-com boom, many consulting firms were merging to achieve greater scale and added capabilities. Caught up in the fervor, Senn Delaney merged with a larger firm in a stock swap. Unfortunately, our merger partner collapsed almost immediately. We lost control of the business, as well as most of the value we'd built over 25 years. And because Senn Delaney was still doing well, our resources were being drained to fund the survival of the larger organization. We had to find a way to buy our firm back, but we knew it would be a major battle.

Just as we were taking on that challenge, I was diagnosed with a cystic acoustic neuroma, a fast-growing tumor on the nerve that connects the ear to the brain. A risky operation was required. In fact, I was told that one slip of the knife could leave the left side of my face permanently paralyzed—not a great prospect for a guy who makes his living in part by talking to groups. And even if the operation was a success, I would probably lose the hearing in my left ear.

As I was trying to absorb those two major blows, my wife came home from the doctor and announced that she was pregnant. This was something we had hoped and prayed for but hadn't expected, since Bernadette was in her fifties and I was in my sixties. Dealing with this dramatic life change at my age—and at the same time as the other two challenges I faced—was a daunting prospect.

I realized that this would be a great test of the principles I had been studying and teaching. I knew that being down the Mood Elevator—feeling worried, depressed, stressed, and resentful—would not give me the wisdom and insight I needed to address these challenges. So how would I rise above the lower mood states?

I made a deliberate, concerted effort to embrace a gratitude perspective. I consciously worked to shake off self-pity and to focus instead on all the blessings I could still appreciate in my life.

Yes, my business faced a significant organizational challenge, but it was still profitable, and my work with client companies and their leaders was still fascinating and fulfilling.

Yes, I had a difficult health problem to address, but the tumor was operable and not life-threatening.

And yes, adding a new family member, especially under such stressful circumstances, would be a difficult adjustment. But our family was a loving and supportive one, and the child on the way represented a blessing for which we had long been praying.

This higher-quality thinking helped me regain access to the wisdom I needed to get through the challenges I faced.

My colleagues and I found a creative way to buy Senn Delaney back, and today our business is stronger and more successful than ever.

A team that included my son Darin did the research to find the surgeon with the best track record in the world for my particular procedure, and somehow we got on his crowded calendar. Prayer groups with hundreds of people spontaneously formed, and I went into the operation with a serenity that was quite remarkable. The operation to remove the brain tumor was a success. And even the downside of the procedure—the lost hearing on my left side—turned out to be a blessing in disguise. I've found that being forced to concentrate on hearing the people around me has made me a better listener overall.

Finally, most wonderful of all, Bernadette gave birth to a beautiful, healthy son who is the joy of our entire family.

Once again I found that an understanding of the Mood Elevator can help with any challenge I face. The biggest lesson I derived from that difficult year was the importance of being grateful for what I have. I don't take my life for granted—and I also don't expect it to be perfect.

Unconditional Gratitude: A Goal to Strive For

Unconditional love is the kind of love a parent has for a child—or the kind of love that people of profound faith have for the higher power in which they believe. It's a love that can never die no matter how circumstances may change.

While I don't know whether it is fully attainable, I aspire to achieve what could be called *unconditional gratitude*. It's a form of gratitude based not on what in my life I am grateful for—the people I love, the work I do, the physical health I enjoy—but rather on life itself, as it is and as it is not.

I think I have experienced unconditional gratitude on occasion. It generally takes the form of a feeling—not a conscious thought but a deep sense of well-being, connected to the awareness that I am part of something bigger and more important than myself. For many people unconditional gratitude has a spiritual quality to it—a knowledge that there is a greater intelligence out there and a desire to attain a deeper understanding of and connection with that intelligence. From that perspective unconditional gratitude might be called a *state of grace*—a gift of great value that is bestowed on us for no apparent reason.

It seems that there are some extraordinary human experiences that make it easier to attain this state of unconditional gratitude.

When astronauts fly 150 to 250 miles above the Earth, they get a view of life that few other humans have seen. They see how thin and fragile the Earth's atmosphere is, how vast the oceans are, how relatively tiny the land mass that humans inhabit is, and how great the destruction is that we've caused to regions like the rain forests. They also see that our planet is a small, single entity floating in endless space, the political boundaries we fight over purely artificial and invisible.

As a result, many astronauts return home with profound changes in perspective. They feel as though they have come closer to seeing the bigger picture—to recognizing the pettiness of the problems we struggle with daily and the richness of the blessings that sustain and unite us. Some embrace pacifism, having come to recognize the foolishness of the battles humans fight and the evil of the political and social divisions we tolerate.

I have a lot for which to be grateful, but like most people I visit the grateful level on the Mood Elevator only from time to time—I don't live there. Yet knowing it is there and accessible to me is a wonderful touchstone that makes my entire life much better.

Honoring Our
Separate Realities

*All the thinkers have had substantially the same
thought. It would probably astound each of them beyond
measure to be let into his neighbor's mind and to find how
different the scenery there was from that in his own.*

—William James

Everyone is familiar with the idiom *Seeing is believing*.
But the more you learn about life, the more you discover
that that simply isn't true. The ease with which our eyes can
deceive us is remarkable.

One powerful illustration of this truth is the surprisingly large number of people falsely convicted of crimes
due to the erroneous testimony of eyewitnesses. In recent
years hundreds of convicted felons have been released from
prison based on the irrefutable results of DNA testing. Some
of these men and women spent decades wrongly incarcerated based on eyewitness accounts—versions of reality that

the witnesses were *absolutely sure* were correct but that turned out to be completely wrong.

In a case from 2011, the Los Angeles chief of police announced with utmost certainty that the department had caught the man who viciously attacked a San Francisco Giants fan after a Dodgers baseball game, putting the fan in a coma—and incensing a city. The arrest was based on seemingly trustworthy eyewitness identification. But a few weeks later, the alleged assailant proved he had been elsewhere, and the police chief was forced to apologize. Only after the innocent man's release was the real perpetrator finally caught.

In criminal cases the fact that seeing is *not* believing can have fatal consequences. But the same truth affects all of us daily in matters big and small. Have you ever driven by something for years without noticing it—perhaps until someone else pointed it out to you? Have you ever been sure you put the car keys one place only to find them somewhere else? Have you ever remembered an incident in one way only to discover, to your astonishment, that another person who was there remembers it very differently?

If any of these experiences sound familiar, it's not because you are unusually careless or absentminded—it's because you are human. All of us have blind spots that affect what we see and don't see. Recognizing and accepting this fact is an important step toward dealing more compassionately and wisely with our fellow humans.

We Live in Separate Realities

Two different people rarely have the exact same thoughts about any topic. In that sense, we live in separate realities.

Here's a small example. To my wife *The Real Housewives of Orange County* is a fascinating television show; it offers a unique glimpse into the lives of some colorful characters, and it helps her appreciate what a great relationship we have in contrast with the dysfunctional ones depicted on the screen.

I couldn't disagree with her more. I find the show painful to watch and utterly without redeeming qualities. It's hard for me to imagine why anyone would want to watch it—least of all someone as intelligent and thoughtful as my Bernadette.

Which one of us is right about *Real Housewives*? Is Bernadette's opinion of the show "correct," or is she "wrong"? That's actually a meaningless question because our judgments about the show are personal, subjective, and based on tastes, interests, and values that are deeply individual; it's inevitable that they will vary from one person to another—and it's impossible to declare either one right or wrong.

Of course, that doesn't stop me from being absolutely convinced that my opinion of *Real Housewives* is "right" and that, in this instance, Bernadette is completely misguided! And I'm sure she feels exactly the same about me in reverse.

This confidence in our own subjective judgments is another inevitable by-product of the human condition.

Each of us has strong filters based on historical thought habits formed by parental influences, the nature of our upbringing, our religious training, our education, our life experiences, and the social settings in which we live. Our perceptions are so thoroughly shaped by these individual forces that it's almost impossible for us to see things otherwise—so we generally go through life utterly convinced that our tastes, preferences, and judgments are "correct," in the same way that eyewitnesses to crimes are convinced of the accuracy of their testimony.

The inevitable clashes that arise between two people based on their differing views of the world may not matter much when the issue is taste in television shows. But when the subject is politics, religion, family finances, business strategy, or other important matters, serious rifts can arise that can threaten the stability of our relationships if we let them. And on the world stage, hatred between groups and communities—and even wars among nations—has been caused by failures to recognize and respect differences in views about life.

A lot of needless conflicts can be avoided if we just remember certain truths about life: that things are not always the way they appear to us; that others inevitably see things differently; that our views and judgments are shaped by our backgrounds and experiences, as are the views and judgments of others; and that it's generally impossible to say who is "right" or "wrong" when matters of opinion and perspective are involved. In short, everyone lives in a separate reality—and the only reasonable thing we can do as mature individuals is to respect those realities.

Based on these truths, one of the fundamental necessities for healthy relationships and a more positive approach to life is a big dose of humility and a studious avoidance of our natural tendency to be judgmental and self-righteous when we disagree with others.

Of course, there are circumstances in which clear boundaries of right and wrong are important and must be respected. Blatant injustice, cruelty, hatred that leads to acts of violence—things like these are evil and must be resisted. But the vast majority of the conflicts of daily life do not rise to that level. Ordinary disagreements are rarely about black and white; much more often they are about shades of gray. And that's where humility and a willingness to accept differing perspectives are crucial.

Being too sure of how you see things and consequently too judgmental and self-righteous produces a range of negative impacts. If the Mood Elevator level labeled *judgmental/ blaming* becomes your unhealthy normal, your experience of life will suffer. You will argue more, be more irritated and bothered, and spend more time feeling angry and defensive. Your lack of understanding of separate realities will cause needless conflicts with people in your life and career.

You are also likely to experience less growth, learning, and discovery. Because you consider yourself the expert on how things are, you will be less open to considering new ideas and fresh ways of seeing things—which means that, over time, your perspective on the world will get narrower and narrower.

Learning to Appreciate the Perspectives of Others

One of the best ways to avoid the narrowness and negativity that goes with being overly fixated on the correctness of your own perception is to cultivate curiosity. (You'll recall that we discussed the importance of curiosity as a Mood Elevator brake back in chapter 5.) When you encounter people or ideas you don't agree with, go to the Mood Elevator level labeled *curious/interested* rather than the levels labeled *judgmental/blaming* or *self-righteous.* Ask yourself, *What is their thinking? Why do they see it differently? How has their background, their experiences, or their education shaped their worldview so that they perceive something I don't perceive?*

It's important to not get sidetracked by questions like *What is the truth? Who is right and who is wrong?* Think not in terms of "truth" but in terms of points of view, of separate realities. Accept the fact that there are multiple versions of every story, many answers to every question, and numerous ways to solve every problem. Remember that you have blind spots—everyone does—and that there is always something new you can learn by listening open-mindedly to the insights of others.

In addition, when communicating your own ideas, change your language to be less dogmatic and certain. Make it clear that what you are saying reflects your personal point of view rather than implying—to others and yourself—that you possess the absolute truth. Here are a few useful qualifiers that can provide you with better ways to state your own perspective:

"It appears to me…"

"The way I see it…"

"From my point of view…"

"I think…" (versus "I know…")

"If I'm not mistaken…"

"I may be wrong, but…"

Finally, as with the other pointers in this book, use your feelings as your guide. When we are overly certain about our opinions and ideas, we tend to experience such feelings as defensiveness, judgment, self-righteousness, and impatience with others. Become acquainted with these emotions and learn to recognize them when they pop up. They are signs that you have stopped listening and learning and instead are shutting out people and possibilities. When this happens, stop talking, sit back, take a deep breath, and try to shift to a mood of curiosity and interest.

Early in my second marriage, the biggest challenge was how to deal with our young children. I wanted desperately for them to know how much I wanted and loved them. That made me a soft touch as a dad and often too short on setting reasonable guidelines.

Bernadette loved the kids, too, but she wanted to help me raise them to be responsible and capable people who could take care of themselves and contribute to our home life.

For a time I approached this disagreement as though it were about who was right and who was wrong. And so long as I viewed the problem through this framing, every suggestion Bernadette offered pushed my emotional buttons. I spent a lot of time being defensive, judgmental, and irritated.

Only when we both understood and accepted the fact that we had different points of view on child raising were we able to blend our approaches, developing a shared way of parenting that combined the best of both styles.

Understanding that in most cases our own self-truth is just our point of view allows us to have healthier relationships. In the wise words of author and educator Stephen Covey, "Seek first to understand, then to be understood."[25]

Avoiding the Blame Game by Assuming Positive Intention

A few years ago, I was boarding a flight at my local airport. In one hand I had my carry-on bag, and in the other was the Orange County section of the *Los Angeles Times*. I'd spotted a feature article in the paper that looked especially interesting, and I was really looking forward to getting seated and reading it.

When I located my seat, I set the paper on it and then looked around for an open space in the overhead bin. Once I'd stowed my bag, I discovered that my paper was no longer on my seat—and I quickly noticed that the man in the seat next to mine was reading the Orange County section of the *Times*.

I immediately dropped my mood to *irritated/bothered* and *judgmental/blaming*. My brain roiled with the thought *The nerve of that guy, helping himself to my paper! And just when I was eager to read it, too.* But I caught myself before dropping to the even lower levels of *self-righteous* and *angry/hostile*. I took a deep breath, reminded myself to not sweat the small stuff, and went to sit down. As soon as I did, I spotted my newspaper: It had fallen to the floor under my seat. The man next to me was reading his *own* copy of the *Times*.

He turned out to be a great guy, and we spent part of the flight enjoying a delightful conversation about the very article that had caught my eye.

Isn't it interesting how quickly our brains jump to blame others and to assume motives for what others do and say, even when there is little or no supporting evidence? Yes, people do the wrong thing sometimes, but in many cases what appears to be a deliberate misdeed—an act of selfishness, dishonesty, or meanness—turns out to be a misunderstanding, minor carelessness, or an innocent mistake. My newspaper story is a small, humorous example, but cases of inferred intent and needless blaming have also led to divorces, lawsuits, ruined careers, political feuds, and even wars.

Sometimes the people we blame for problems are completely innocent of any wrongdoing, as was the case with my seatmate on the plane. Other times they may have committed the act we blame them for, but with extenuating circumstances that dramatically lessen their degree of guilt.

I heard a story once about an avid nature-lover and conservationist who was on a trip to Yosemite National Park. Pulling into a parking spot near a camping area, he noticed a woman drop a bag of garbage on the ground right next to the trash can. Incensed at this act of carelessness, the man jumped from his car and ran over to vent his irritation—only to notice that the woman was carrying a red and white cane. She was blind and had proudly, and with some difficulty, found the trash can but accidentally missed on the drop.

How many of the things that drive us to the *judgmental/blaming* floor on the Mood Elevator involve similar, inadvertent mistakes? People cut off other drivers when changing lanes on the freeway because they don't realize how close the other cars are. A work project doesn't get completed on time because an important supply delivery was delayed when an order form got lost in the mail. A casual office joke about "annoying in-laws" is perceived as a cruelly insensitive remark by someone whose deeply beloved father-in-law just passed away after a long illness— unbeknownst to her joking co-worker.

All of us have said and done things we regret, especially when we are caught up in low-level thinking. When we are in low-mood states like *worried/anxious, defensive/insecure,* or *stressed/burned-out,* we lose some of our emotional intelligence. We may become socially inept and oblivious to the impact we are having on others. The question is, *Can those affected by the mistakes we make have the wisdom to understand the underlying causes and shrug off the experience—or do they take it personally, perhaps escalating a small misunderstanding into a bitter, lasting conflict?*

On a business trip, I arrived at my hotel quite late at night as a result of a long-delayed flight. I was greeted by one of the most surly, unfriendly desk clerks I have ever encountered. After initially declaring (incorrectly) that I had no reservation, he reluctantly checked me in, all the while complaining about the weather, the city, and having to work late—none of which was of interest to me; I just wanted to check in and go to my room.

It would have been easy for me to become irritated and tell him, "Just do your job and stop bothering me." Instead, for some reason I'm not quite certain of, I went up a few levels on the Mood Elevator to *patient/understanding* with a touch of compassion. I found myself feeling sorry for this man whose life seemed so grim. I felt a sense of gratitude for my life compared with his and for the understanding I had that allows me to enjoy it so much. I ended up sympathizing with the clerk about his tough day. "It must be hard," I remarked. "I'd hate to have to work this late."

The clerk's attitude immediately improved. He handed me my room key with a smile and wished me a successful visit in his city. Most importantly, the encounter didn't ruin my evening. Instead it provided me with another example of how a commitment to living among the higher floors on the Mood Elevator can make your life better.

Making a Fresh Start

Problems like conflicting perspectives, judgment, and blaming don't arise only in personal relationships; they pose problems for many business organizations as well. That's why, as part of our corporate training process, Senn Delaney urges leadership teams to assume positive intentions in teammates. One way to practice this is to think about what we call a *fresh start*. It's a way of getting past a history of conflict, misunderstanding, or mistrust and moving toward a better, more hopeful future.

Once we have given the team a deeper understanding and experience of the role of thought and the Mood Elevator, we remind them that whatever happened in the past exists now only in memory. Therefore probably little can be done to rectify any friction or trust issues that developed in the past. The healthiest path is to let go of that history and judge one another on how they work together going forward, with their new level of understanding of the principle of life effectiveness.

To enable this, team members must accept the fact that they will see things differently based on their varied points of view. They also need to assume positive intentions in one another. After all, our assumptions determine our reactions to what other people say and do:

▶ If we assume that someone else's action was spiteful and personal, we will feel justified in being outraged and seeking revenge.

▶ If we assume that someone else's action was intentional, we will feel justified in being angry and expressing that through our own words and deeds.

▶ If we assume that someone else's action was caused by gross negligence or apathy, we will feel justified in judging it harshly.

▶ If we assume that someone else's action was unintentional but that they should have known better, we will feel justified in being irritated and bothered.

But...

▶ If we assume that the other person lacked information, was uninformed, and just did what made sense to them, we can be understanding and patient and work toward a solution.

▶ If we assume and accept that the other person was in a low mood state when they behaved as they did, we can handle the issue with grace, avoid personalizing it, and wait for the right time to resolve the resulting issues.

Notice that the underlying action from past history remains the same; the crucial variable is the spin we put on it. Our assumptions can generate emotions that reflect the full range of the Mood Elevator, from anger and hostility to understanding and appreciation. The choice is ours.

A fresh start requires that we consciously choose to make positive assumptions about one another. When a fresh start is entered into in the right spirit and at the right time, it can revitalize relationships within a group.

The notion of a fresh start can play a powerful role in mending any relationship—at work or in your personal life. We can't fix the past, but we can move past it and start anew. Sometimes that's the only way to rebuild a damaged relationship.

Seeing Innocence as a Key to Forgiveness

Moving past injuries and hurts of the past can be very hard to do, especially when you genuinely feel that you were wronged. Even if the person who hurt you has apologized, the incident may stay in your thinking and affect your mood, especially when something happens to remind you of it.

I was out running early one morning while on an East Coast business trip. I needed a few minutes of quiet before a busy day with a client. I also had something on my mind that was bothering me—something someone had done that I couldn't seem to let go of. As I ran, the memory gnawed at me, making it hard for me to experience the serenity and openness I usually enjoy when I exercise.

I saw an open door of a church. I looked inside, and no one was there. It was peaceful and quiet, with beautiful stained-glass windows. I decided to go inside and see whether different surroundings could help change my mood.

As I sat in one of the pews to relax, I looked up and saw a large statue of Jesus on the cross with the phrase *Forgive them for they know not what they do* etched below. Somehow those words struck me quite powerfully that day. If Jesus could forgive those who killed him, who was I to hang on to small slights and resentments?

Depending on circumstances, there are many ways to rephrase that sentiment:

▶ Forgive them, for they were in a low mood state, and their low-quality thinking drove their actions.

▶ Forgive them, for they saw things differently than I did.

▶ Forgive them, for they didn't know how important it was to me.

▶ Forgive them, for they didn't realize they were hurting me.

When we understand the role of thought in shaping our attitudes and behaviors, it's easier to see innocence in those around us. Remember that everyone does what makes sense to them based on their thinking. When someone hurts you, disappoints you, or angers you, the cause is rarely personal; it's unlikely that they are deliberately seeking to injure you. They are just doing what follows from their thinking. In this sense, they are innocent, and forgiveness is an appropriate response.

This doesn't mean that you should refuse to recognize the bad behavior of others, particularly when it involves a pattern of dishonest, hurtful, or unethical actions. In chapter 4 I explained how Senn Delaney turned down the opportunity to work with Enron because of the company's history of ruthless behavior—particularly since the company's leaders told us they saw nothing wrong with their policies and in fact intended to double down on them. Our decision wasn't based on a feeling of condemnation toward the executives at Enron for being "bad people"—just that it was not a company with which we felt comfortable working. This is the kind of judgment anyone may need to make, and it's a different matter from nursing anger or resentment over the misdeeds of others.

I also don't mean to imply that you should allow people to take advantage of you, use you, or abuse you; but whenever possible, you *should* try to see the innocence in others, if only for your own benefit. When you can see others' actions without inferring intent on their part, you won't take things personally and will maintain your bearings. You keep your mental traction, avoid intense emotional reactions, and position yourself to respond to challenges and problems with clarity of vision, insight, and wisdom.

The long-term result is a better quality of life and more-satisfying, meaningful relationships.

By contrast, when you assume nefarious motives and ill intentions on the part of other people and hold on to resentment over past injuries, you are the one who suffers. The other person may not even know or care that you are feeling hurt and angry, but it is *your* quality of life that will deteriorate as you spend more time in the lower mood states.

Learning to assume the innocence in others is a powerful way to spend more of your time up the Mood Elevator, at home, in your community, and at work.

13

Nurturing Faith and Optimism

I have learned that some of the nicest people you'll ever meet are those who have suffered a traumatic event or loss. I admire them for their strength, but most especially for their life gratitude—a gift often taken for granted by the average person in society.

—Sasha Azevedo

Living life up the Mood Elevator greatly depends on how you react when you face adversity. Life happens—including seemingly bad things. It is what you make of those things in your thinking and the path you choose in response that determines your quality of life.

Marilyn Hamilton came back from adversity stronger and more purposeful. Growing up in Fresno, California, Marilyn had it all: a loving family and good looks (she was a beauty queen). She was also an accomplished athlete and an adventurous spirit who eventually journeyed to Australia to teach school. But one fateful day, while hang-gliding near her hometown, she neglected to correctly fasten her linch-pin to her harness. She crashed into the side of a mountain and woke up a paraplegic, paralyzed from the waist down.

"I realized I was in trouble when, at the rehab center, I tried to sit up and immediately fell to the side like a ragdoll," Marilyn said. Weeks of physical therapy followed. The only way she could move around was in a wheelchair. "People looked at me with pity, like I was sick, but I wasn't sick. I was the same Marilyn, just with a different mode of getting around in the world."[26]

Marilyn was distressed to discover that even the best wheelchairs then available were, as she called them, "steel dinosaurs." She decided to do something about it. Marilyn and her hang-gliding buddies set up shop in a garage in Fresno and designed an entirely new wheelchair using the same aerodynamic materials found in hang-gliders. These chairs were lightweight, fast, maneuverable, and flexible, with parts that could be adjusted to fit the user's body and specific disability needs. They jazzed them up, painting them pink and purple and other vibrant colors. They even decorated Marilyn's new chair with rhinestones and named it The Quickie. What they did was much bigger than giving Marilyn a fun, sexy chair that reflected her personality; for people with disabilities, they changed the world forever.

Today, Quickie brand wheelchairs are sold around the world, and one of Marilyn's original wheelchairs is showcased in the Smithsonian Institution in Washington, DC. Marilyn has gone on to win numerous medals for wheelchair sports, including US Open tennis tournaments and skiing competitions. She has been featured on network television shows, including *60 Minutes,* and has testified before Congress. She received the Minerva Award at Maria Shriver's Women's Conference in 2006 and is known the world over as a spokesperson for people with disabilities.

Marilyn observed, "It is not what happens to you in life that molds you; rather, it is how you respond. My motto is, *If you can't stand up, stand out.*" Marilyn is a wonderful example of the central theme of this book—that life is what you make of it through your thinking.

Seeking the Right Outcome

In many religions, people are taught the practice of *petitionary prayer*—asking for a specific outcome: good health, relief from pain, a solution to a problem. Many have found this kind of petitionary prayer a meaningful part of their spiritual lives. But I was taught by my mother to pray instead for the "right outcome." In essence, the prayer is for the right path to be revealed—that we will have the wisdom to see, do, and say the right things and make the best decisions we can. Woven into this form of prayer is the assumption that we don't always know what's best for us. In fact, it's often unclear whether what's happening to us is bad or good; time teaches us that many events that appear harmful are blessings in disguise.

There's an old Eastern tale about an elderly farmer whose entire family is economically dependent on the farmer's hardworking son. When the son breaks his leg, it is seen as a major disaster—until the emperor's guards come to the village to round up all the able-bodied young men to fight in a distant war from which many will not return. Suddenly, the son's temporary disability is revealed as a great gift.

I've learned from personal experience that seemingly disastrous events can turn out to be blessings.

As I recounted earlier, the end of my first marriage was the most painful thing that had ever happened to me. But the self-reflection it triggered led to a new life that is better than I could have imagined. I was driven to reflect on what was really important to me and what my purpose on earth was. I realized that I had been taking my three young sons—Kevin, Darin, and Jason, then ages seven, five, and three—for granted. The time I spent with them was more dutiful than wholehearted. Thanks to my new, clearer perspective, my central focus changed to building closer, more unconditionally loving relationships with them.

That whole process jolted me out of a world of distorted priorities, unconscious habits, and unhealthy normal. I began a journey to get to know myself and to discover deeper meaning in my life. Without the wakeup call of that painful divorce, that wouldn't have occurred.

The experience also caused me to challenge my beliefs and behaviors and to see more possibilities for myself as an evolving human being. It led me to change the direction of my career and ultimately to found Senn Delaney as a culture-shaping firm that embodies my true mission in life.

Many people respond to an adverse event or circumstance by asking, "Why did that happen to me?" This path of questioning leads to lower mood states marked by blame, judgment, and even depression. Instead, when painful things happen to you, try asking, "Why did that happen *for* me?" This less-traveled path positions you not as a passive victim but as an active person, seeking the path to your own right outcome. It lifts you higher up the Mood Elevator, prompting curiosity, resourcefulness, and optimism.

The Power of Faith

Imagine what it would be like to know that, no matter how serious the problems you now face, in the end everything will work out okay. Imagine knowing that even if a close friend or loved one does something to hurt you, your love will prevail and you will be close again. Imagine going through a seemingly disastrous day confident in the knowledge that this too shall pass.

What I'm describing here is the gift of *faith*. Faith gives you hope and wisdom. It makes you less likely to catastrophize—to waste time and energy imagining all the terrible things that *could* happen. Instead it allows you to focus your resources on developing creative solutions to whatever problems you face.

When my daughter was attending business school at the University of Southern California, she asked me why she had to take a complex math course for which she could see no possible use in her career. I shared with her one of my theories about the purpose of college: Yes, it is to educate, but more than that it is to demonstrate that problems that seem difficult or even impossible to solve *can* be solved. Experiencing this repeatedly helps us develop the faith that we'll be able to solve the next seemingly insoluble problem that comes along. It's an important lesson to learn, whether you learn it in college or in life's own school of hard knocks.

Faith can take many different forms:

▶ Faith in your own competence or ability

▶ Faith that you will find a way through the day's darkness of difficulty

▶ Faith that you can handle the future no matter what it brings

▶ Faith that your natural state is a healthy one and that it can return if you lose it

▶ Faith in God or some higher intelligence or power that is greater than you and I

In a way, it doesn't matter which of these forms of faith you find most intuitively appealing. What matters is that you believe in something that gives you hope and confidence for the future. Faith as described here is not passive; it's not a matter of waiting around and hoping for the best. In fact, it is just the opposite: It is a very active process that liberates all the energy, creativity, and resourcefulness inside you. Faith frees us from the paralysis that depression and despair can bring. When we live in faith, we see more options and discover more solutions to whatever problems life throws our way.

Faith played an important role in my making it through college. I applied to engineering school in the late 1950s, right after Russia sent *Sputnik 1,* the first artificial Earth satellite, into space, sparking an international competition for scientific and engineering talent. Schools like the University of California, Los Angeles (UCLA), were inundated with engineering applications. They set extremely high acceptance standards and still had to wash out two-thirds of the freshman class who simply didn't have the grit to survive. I went from being a top student in my small high school to feeling like one of the dumbest of the exceptionally brainy kids in my class at UCLA.

I can still remember the calculus class that started every day at noon, with the bells of Royce Hall tolling ominously in the background. One day our stern, elderly professor ordered me to the blackboard to solve a complex problem just after the bell stopped ringing: "Senn—problem three in the homework." As I struggled to solve the equation, he was right beside me, erasing my work and shaking his head in disgust and pity. After a few moments, he stopped me and suggested I consider changing my major or dropping the class.

I went home that weekend and told my mother I didn't think I could make it. Thankfully, Mom didn't let me succumb to despair. Instead she sat me down and talked to me in a very supportive and affirming way. She said I had all the God-given qualities I needed to succeed in school and in life. I had been created whole, complete, and capable—I just had to believe it. Mom concluded by paraphrasing the promise of Jesus: If you have faith the size of a mustard seed, you can move mountains.

I learned later that Jesus was referring to the black mustard plant, an annual that grows up to 9 feet tall yet starts from a very tiny seed. If something so huge grows from such a humble beginning, maybe I could build a successful college career from the frail start I'd experienced so far.

My mother also told me that the only thing that could stop me was my own thinking. She gave me a copy of a little book called *As a Man Thinketh* by James Allen. Originally published in 1902, it begins:

> Mind is the Master power that moulds and makes,
> And Man is Mind, and evermore he takes
> The tool of Thought, and, shaping what he wills,
> Brings forth a thousand joys, a thousand ills:—
> He thinks in secret, and it comes to pass:
> Environment is but his looking-glass.[27]

I carried around Allen's little book for years. Here are a few other useful concepts I took from it:

▶ Every action and feeling is preceded by a thought.

▶ Right thinking begins with the words we say to ourselves.

▶ Circumstance does not make the man; it reveals him to himself.

I'm sure you can recognize the lifelong influence of James Allen's thinking on my own approach to life, as reflected in this book.

I did finish engineering school, though I later realized that my passion wasn't for engineering but rather for working in business with people. I went on to get my MBA, fell in love with solving business case study problems, and discovered that I wanted a career in consulting.

The True Meaning of Faith

Let's be clear about what I am advocating when I urge you to live a life filled with faith, hope, and optimism. It is not about "the power of positive thinking." We all ride the Mood Elevator from top to bottom, and we can't have positive thoughts all the time. What we *can* do is pay attention to our feelings as a guide to the quality of our thinking. When we do, we can hold our negative thoughts more lightly and take them less seriously. As a result, they will have less power over us and we will function better.

I am not endorsing being naïvely optimistic. There is a wise Sufi saying: *Trust in God and tie your camel.* In other words, have faith and hope—but at the same time be realistic, plan for contingencies, and be prepared, proactive, and accountable.

I am not recommending that you get carried away with exuberance and unbridled excitement. Just as it is best to not make decisions when you are low on the Mood Elevator, it is also important to not make decisions when you are euphoric with an overactive mind. That behavior has led to many spur-of-the-moment Las Vegas weddings that didn't work out and many valueless timeshares and condos purchased by people enjoying a relaxing vacation.

Strange as it may seem, wild enthusiasm has much the same impact on the clarity of our thinking as do anxiety or anger. All are intense feelings that *seem* compelling and that are accompanied by a loud internal voice justifying the action you want to take. Don't confuse emotions like elation and exuberance with higher mood states like gratitude, wisdom, and creativity. Faith, hope, and genuine optimism evoke a more serene feeling—the product of a quiet mind.

Few things can enhance our experience of life more than faith and hope. We all will face difficult situations and challenging people in our lives. The healthiest and least stressful way to deal with them is with a good measure of faith and hope. So wherever faith originates for you, cherish it and nourish it, even in the most difficult times. It will serve you well.

Dealing With Your Down Days

Happiness is not the absence of problems—
it's the ability to deal with them.

—STEVE MARABOLI

The **primary goal** of this book is to provide tips and pointers that can help you spend more time up the Mood Elevator. But we will all spend time among the lower floors as well, since having low moods is a natural, normal part of life. That's why a secondary goal of this book is to help you do less damage to yourself and others when you are feeling down.

As sentient beings, possessing the power of thought and emotions is a gift that advances us intellectually. This allows us to imagine the future, plan for things yet to come, muse about possibilities, and analyze and interpret everything that is going on within and around us. Thought has allowed us to conquer polio, write timeless classical music, and travel to the moon.

That same power to imagine through thought can also cause us to worry excessively and unnecessarily, experience periods of depression about real or imagined problems, have moments of paranoia based on our assumptions about others' motives, be self-righteous and judgmental, and even experience fits of anger and rage. No matter how well you understand the principles in this book, your thinking will at times take you to the lower levels on the Mood Elevator. That's why learning to *do down well* is a necessary skill.

Remember That Your Thinking Is Unreliable in Low Mood States

Have you ever said something to a friend or loved one in the heat of the moment that you wished you could take back? Have you ever hit the *send* button to transmit an email that you later realized was a terrible mistake? If either of these has happened to you, think back to the circumstances. Where were you on the Mood Elevator map when this occurred? Most likely, you were somewhere in the lower half.

Both of these examples illustrate the most important principle in dealing effectively with down days: remember that your thinking is unreliable in the lower mood states, so don't trust it; try not to act on it right away. Instead question and challenge your thinking before relying on it as a guide to action.

When I get an email that pushes my buttons, dropping me into a state of irritation, anxiety, or anger, I *may* type a response—but then I will click *save to draft* rather than the *send* button. I allow several hours or even a day to pass. By the time I read my reply again, I am usually at a different level on the Mood Elevator, and I can see the flawed thinking it contains. Sometimes I delete the response and start over; other times I'll thoroughly edit the message to take out the irritation and judgment before finally hitting *send*.

As for the things we may say to a loved one while in a low-mood state, those are a little harder to control than emails. Technology doesn't come to our rescue in this case. Instead you need to learn to be very deliberate in your communication style—to avoid saying or doing hurtful things in times of stress and low-quality thinking.

Bernadette and I first got together in the 1970s, the era of the human potential movement. The conventional relationship wisdom at the time was encapsulated in sayings like *Tell it like it is, Let it all hang out,* and *Don't go to bed with anything left unsaid.* As a result, there were a few times when we struggled unproductively until all hours of the night, fighting over issues that, in retrospect, were usually not worth the time and energy.

As we both began to better understand how our minds worked, Bernadette suggested a new ground rule: let's not take on any significant relationship issue when either of us is on any of the lower levels on the Mood Elevator. The impact of that rule has been quite remarkable. It is one reason why we have such a peaceful, loving, respectful relationship today. We take on critical issues and deal with them honestly and forthrightly—but we do so only when we are both in the higher mood states.

If you're wondering how we follow and enforce this ground rule, a typical dialog between us might go like this:

> LARRY: It looks like you are feeling bothered about something. Is it something you want to talk about?
>
> BERNADETTE: No, not now. My thinking is not clear. If I need to talk about it, I'll let you know later.

Bernadette may wait a few hours or even a day to see how she feels about the issue when she is back up the Mood Elevator. She may find that the issue simply dissolves in the light of her higher-quality thinking. Or she may find that she needs to talk about it with me. In that case, the issue is usually dealt with very easily and in an almost "by the way" manner.

I must admit I was alarmed at first because all the drama went out of our relationship. I now see that the practice has led to the special loving, supportive relationship we have without the all-too-common arguing and bickering many couples get caught up in.

Low Mood State: Drive with Caution!

As I mentioned earlier, our teenage son, Logan, somehow understands this concept best of all. He has a leg up because he naturally tends to have a quiet mind, but like all of us he has an occasional meltdown—a time when he is overwhelmed with homework or just having a bad day. When he does, he tells us, "Just leave me alone. Don't try to talk to me now because I won't hear you anyway and I may say something I really don't mean. Just let me go to my room until I'm back to the real me. Then I'll come out again." Many adults could benefit from a similar approach to their moods.

One of our consultants at Senn Delaney came up with a great analogy for *doing down well.* Suppose you *must* drive somewhere on a very dark, cold, snowy night with an icy road. You'll do it—but with great caution. You'll drive slowly, take turns gently, and leave plenty of space between you and any other drivers or objects on the road.

Apply the same kind of caution to your communications with others when you're stuck in a low mood. Remember that your instincts are not right. This is not a good time to tell someone what you *really* think of them, or to make an important life decision, or to tackle a major problem. Wait until your healthy normal reemerges among the upper floors on the Mood Elevator; then you will find that you can deal with issues much more easily, quickly, and painlessly.

Using the Mood Elevator as your guide and not acting on low-level thoughts and impulses when you are feeling down is one of the key principles to doing less damage to yourself—and to others.

15

Relationships and the Mood Elevator

*Things turn out best for people who make
the best of the way things turn out.*

—ANONYMOUS

As you've seen, many of the concepts described in this
book—from mild preference to separate realities to seeing
innocence—can be used to foster better relationships at
work and more-loving relationships at home. And when
it comes to building relationships, nowhere is the Mood
Elevator more helpful. That's because our connection to
others and to the world depends on how well we manage
the up-and-down ride.

When we are down, we feel alone. We feel discon-
nected. We tend not to reach out to others or be supportive
of them. When we are in the lower mood states, people
bother us more easily. We are more judgmental of others
and tend to assume ulterior motives behind what they do
and say. Irritation, bother, judgment, and anger are not good

places to be in when you are trying to foster supportive, collaborative relationships.

But it's a different story altogether in the higher mood states because a healthy state of mind and healthy relationships are related.

There is a notion in Eastern philosophy of keeping your karma clean. My simple interpretation of that: go out of your way to make more friends and no enemies, and life will somehow go better.

In the business world, we often talk about the importance of collaboration and teamwork. But all too many organizations have an us-versus-them mentality, trust issues, a lack of cooperation between different departments, strained relationships between the corporate office and the field organizations, and other social dysfunctions.

Relationship issues also exist in families, of course. While there are countless loving and supportive couples and families, there are also myriad dysfunctional ones. There are siblings who don't forgive one another for years or even decades for minor slights, in-laws who are considered outlaws, and couples who constantly bicker.

It is easy to see how relationships are tied to the Mood Elevator. Who wants to be around someone who spends too much time on the lower levels, feeling and behaving depressed, self-righteous, judgmental, bothered, or angry?

On the other hand, isn't it energizing to be with people who are more often on the higher mood levels, feeling and behaving hopeful, appreciative, optimistic, and understanding? Wouldn't you rather be with someone who has a sense of humor than someone who is mostly just irritable?

In the upper mood states, people are willing and able to commit to a higher purpose, such as family, community, or service; in the lower states, it is "all about me." It is easy to see how concern for the greater good builds healthy, sustainable relationships at work and at home.

When we are concerned about and interested in others and are willing to play win-win in a more unselfish way, we develop those strong relationships. But if it is "all about me" and we view the world through a win/lose lens, our relationships suffer.

The Luck Factor

Relationship skills are a foundation for a more successful and fulfilling life. Years ago I read a little book by Richard Wiseman called *The Luck Factor: The Four Essential Principles*. It describes a series of theories about the concept of luck. The theory that most resonated with me was that "lucky" people have a much wider and stronger network of supportive relationships.

The example I recall is a woman who got the dream job she never expected would be offered. When researchers traced the job offer back, they found that the woman had built a network of very supportive people who "showed up" as she sought the job. Thanks to this network, her references were glowing, her letters of recommendation were strong, and (unbeknownst to her) there were people she knew who knew people within the organization who came forward in her support.

"Luck," then, is not a random factor that lands on some people for no apparent reason. It's an outgrowth of healthy relationships. People who better manage their Mood Elevators have far more connections and support systems than those who don't. That is why their lives seem to work out better—and why they even seem to be "luckier" than others.

To foster good relationships, let your feelings be your guide: look for and cultivate feelings of understanding, compassion, love, and warmth toward others. This is often hardest to do with those closest to us because they are often the ones who can most easily push our buttons.

It takes conscious awareness to assume good intentions (not self-centered motives) in loved ones, to see their innocence, and to be willing to forgive the times they've hurt or disappointed us. Accepting the idiosyncrasies of others, particularly loved ones, and honoring their right to a separate, different reality is one key to healthy, loving relationships.

Most of us spend the majority of our lives in relationships with parents, our children, other loved ones, and co-workers. Understanding how to spend more time among the upper floors on the relationship Mood Elevator greatly improves our quality of life and that of those around us.

Pointers for Riding the Mood Elevator

*The happiness of your life depends on
the quality of your thoughts.*

—MARCUS AURELIUS

Living life up the Mood Elevator and at your best is based on a few fundamental premises.

Life happens, and it's not always pretty, but we have the choice to make of life what we will through our thinking. The first premise of living life up the Mood Elevator is to understand that our thinking creates our experience of life—and we have the power to direct it as we will.

The second premise is that we came into this world with what could be called *innate health*. That includes the whole system that gives us the ability to experience life through our thoughts and feelings. It also represents a set of built-in, inborn, God-given traits, including the fact that we are naturally loving, curious, and wise. Our innate health represents all the higher levels on the Mood Elevator.

Over time we all develop thought habits and unhealthy-normal thinking that takes us away from our natural state. This is inevitable because our thinking triggers our feelings, and our thinking varies from moment to moment and can be influenced by many things.

The teachings I have shared in this book are designed to help connect you to your innate health—the best of who you already are at your core. In some sense, you don't have to learn anything other than how to access that innate health, but to do that requires an understanding of the role of thought and the feelings that it generates. Only you can learn to ride the Mood Elevator in your own unique way, just as only you could learn to walk, beginning with those first few wobbly steps as a baby.

The pointers in this book will help you do just that:

▶ Know that at your core you have innate health and the ability to be at your best. This is a very reassuring idea—one you can turn to in times of doubt and anxiety.

▶ Know that to be human means you will ride the Mood Elevator and visit each and every floor.

▶ Look to your feelings as your guide to tell you when you are down the Mood Elevator. Carry a Mood Elevator pocket card as a daily reminder.

▶ Learn to recognize the feelings that accompany any unhealthy-normal thinking or thought patterns, and make them a loud bell.

▶ Use pattern interrupts to change your thinking and your feelings.

▶ Feed the thoughts you favor, not those that drop you to the lower floors on the Mood Elevator.

▶ Live in the world of mild preference—not a world of "have-to's" and "my ways."

▶ Take better care of yourself and remember to stretch and recover with exercise, sleep, and time off.

▶ Use breathing and self-awareness exercises to *be here now* and quiet your mind.

▶ Maintain a gratitude perspective; count your blessings daily and be grateful for life itself.

▶ Recognize and honor the separate realities we all live in. Be quick to understand others' perspectives and slow to blame or criticize.

▶ Remember that your thinking is unreliable in the lower mood states, so delay important conversations and decisions; don't act on your unreliable thinking, and don't take your lower mood state out on other people.

▶ Have faith that when you are down the Mood Elevator, this too shall pass—just like the weather. The sun is always up there; the clouds can obscure it, but they will pass, as will your low mood.

The greatest gift I received as a child was the message from my mother that my natural state was to be loving, wise, and capable—that I was born whole and complete and that anytime I doubted that, it was just an error in my thinking. My goal is to "pay it forward."

My hope is that the concepts in this book can put you on a path to finding that key and creating more love, joy, peace, inspiration, fulfillment, and success in your life.

How This Book Came to Be

The **acknowledgments page** gives credit to those who have had an impact on this book, but it doesn't tell the story of where the concepts came from and the roles that different people played. This section is for anyone who has an interest in that story.

Many of the notions in this book came to me through the school of life; that is, I learned them by reflecting on my own personal experiences and through the work that Senn Delaney has done to enable thriving organizational cultures for clients around the world. Other notions are my personal interpretation of concepts I've learned from some very progressive teachers in the field of mental health who first discovered and translated these principles.

Almost 20 years ago, my friend Paul Nakai asked my wife and me to attend a lecture by a gentleman named Sydney Banks (whom you may recall I mentioned in chapter 4). Syd is the person I consider the originator of the core principles underlying the concepts in this book. He was a simple tradesman who one day had an epiphany—a flash of insight about the fact that his entire experience of life was the result of his thinking. He was touched by the notion that human beings were given the power of thought through which to experience life—and that we experience it largely through our feelings or consciousness.

Syd had a simple but very touching way of communicating these profound notions, and he began to attract a following. My wife and I attended his one-day presentation on the campus of the University of California, Berkeley. It was just two 2-hour segments, with ample breaks, during which Syd sat in a chair and talked about three principles: mind, consciousness, and thought. Though we didn't fully grasp his ideas (in fact, we didn't even understand many of them!), we did come away from the lecture seeing life a little differently. We also felt noticeably different. We had an improved experience of life for many weeks afterward: we were more patient, tolerant, peaceful, and loving. Life somehow just looked better.

We were struck by the fact that people who were understanding these principles on a deeper level were reporting better relationships with family and loved ones, increased creativity, improved peace of mind, new resourcefulness, greater career effectiveness, and more gratitude for life.

Bernadette, who at the time was head of Human Resources, including training and development, for Senn Delaney, concluded that there might be some concepts in Syd's message that could help us in our work with clients. Senn Delaney's goal has always been to foster healthy, high-performing teams and organizational cultures.

An important aspect of that work is the seminars we conduct to connect our clients with a set of essential values and principles for life effectiveness. Bernadette reasoned that this might be another avenue to connect people to the best of who they really are.

At about the same time, we were introduced to another healthcare professional—George S. Pransky, PhD—who had also become intrigued with Syd Banks's message. George decided to give up his traditional practice as a psychologist in the San Francisco Bay Area and move to a small town north of Seattle to start a mental health practice to help individuals understand Syd's concepts.

If Bernadette and I were ever going to teach those principles, we had to learn to use them ourselves, so we decided to spend a week with George to see what we could learn. What was interesting was that he had developed a wellness practice rather than a mental illness practice. Most psychotherapy is about "fixing people." The goal of George's practice—and our goal, as well—was to take people who were already successful by the world's standards and help them be even more effective and lead more fulfilling lives.

I began thinking about what might make *me* even more effective. What would enhance my experience of life? At the time things were going quite well. Senn Delaney was successful. My kids were doing fine. My relationship with Bernadette, while not perfect, was very good and improving with every year.

Upon reflection there were definitely things that detracted from my effectiveness and my quality of life. One I was aware of was the fact that I was wound pretty tight. I took my work and most everything else too seriously. I had a very busy mind and lived at a level of impatience and intensity on what I know today as the Mood Elevator.

Occasionally, when I would take a vacation that lasted more than a week and allow my mind the time to quiet down, I would catch a glimpse of a very different kind of life—one where I was more appreciative of nature and people, where I lived in the present moment more often, where I was a better listener, where I experienced greater peace. But those moments were fleeting and exceptional. As a result, I wasn't always the best listener—and in my haste to move forward, I would often finish other people's sentences. That was definitely something I could work on.

Another aspect of my life I realized I could work on, which was even more compelling (and more draining), was what I now understand to be my worry habit. Even though my life was going quite well, I had a tendency to fill my mind too often with anxious thoughts.

Worry became the perfect topic because it is the ideal example of how we live through our thinking. When we worry about something and start spinning all of our scenarios, it's as if the event actually happened. We have all the physical, psychological, and emotional consequences of the event—even though it hasn't actually occurred.

In reality, most of what we worry about never happens, and the things that do occur are rarely as significant as we make them out to be in our own minds. That got me thinking about how much better my quality of life would have been if I'd merely not worried about those things that ended up never happening. I urge you to ponder that same thought.

My time with George Pransky proved invaluable; it showed me that feelings of worry and intensity were so much a part of my habit that they were a blind spot for me. Because I didn't notice them, I couldn't do much about them. As a result of my newfound understanding, I began to value a quieter mind and more peaceful feelings. Feelings of excessive intensity and worry became more like loud bells—and those unhealthy thought habits diminished greatly.

As a result of continuing to deepen my understanding of the role of thought and incorporating the principles that I learned from George into my life, I'm happy to report that today I have a far more peaceful life with far less intensity and worry. I've become acutely aware of the feelings that go along with worry, so I recognize them when I go there on the Mood Elevator. Sometimes all it takes to snap me out of worry is a simple, gentle admonition to myself, such as *There you go again.* This reminds me to be accountable for possible outcomes but not to create a soap opera in my head about it.

That early work with George, coupled with what I have learned since, has led me to the kind of relationship with my wife that is beyond what I could have imagined. It is continually fresh, loving, supportive, forgiving, stress-free, and passionate—yet amazingly peaceful.

The impact these concepts have had on our five children, however, may be the most powerful gift I have received. That gift—and a desire to help others live life at their best—led to my developing the Mood Elevator as a tool and discovering the secrets of riding it consciously.

This positive personal experience set me on the path to better understand how to use these principles in my own life and to incorporate them into the work Senn Delaney does with business leaders around the world. It took years of trial and error in coaching executives and leading seminars to find easy ways to help people understand the Mood Elevator and how to ride it better. It took additional years to explore the research and science governing our moods and to write this book. Today the Mood Elevator has become a foundational aspect of our corporate seminars. It is an integral part of the sessions we conduct to support personal change, which is one aspect of shaping an organization's culture.

In doing this work with organizations, I have seen the Mood Elevator embraced by employees—from the CEO to frontline associates—in more than 100 of the Fortune 500 organizations in the United States and dozens of Global 1000 firms around the world. We have also had great acceptance of the concept by major institutions like universities, hospitals, and city and state governments. People from almost every nation, language, and level easily relate to the Mood Elevator and are able to use it as a guide to enhance their own lives.

We have devised simple, commonsense ways to connect people with the principles and give them practical pointers to riding the Mood Elevator with greater ease. We have also developed a large body of knowledge about the things that can (and do) affect our moods. People who use these pointers report that they are living life at their best more often and with more success and less stress. This book is designed to bring a deeper understanding to those who have some familiarity with the concept through our seminars and to introduce the Mood Elevator to a far broader audience, as well.

Notes

1. I use the word *thoughts* to refer to all the mental reactions we experience in response to the events of our lives—not just the rational, logical analysis we sometimes describe as "thinking." The thoughts that drive our moods include memories, plans, fantasies, worries, regrets, anticipations, fears, desires, and much more. All are "happenings in your head"—thoughts of various kinds that have a profound impact on your mood.

2. Les Wexner, June 13, 2013, personal communication with the author.

3. Yum Brands: David Novak, CEO & Chairman, "Aligning 1.4 million employees," *CEO Show* interview, February 5, 2012.

4. Joe Robles, April 2012, personal communication with the author.

5. "Three Principles: Well-Being Solutions for Life," http://www .threeprinciplestraining.com/page/history-three-principles.

6. David Lieberman, "CEO Forum: Microsoft's Ballmer Having a 'Great Time,'" *USA Today,* April 30, 2007.

7. Kevin Freiberg, *Nuts! Southwest Airline's Crazy Recipe for Business and Personal Success* (New York: Doubleday, 1998).

8. Ann Pietrangelo, "The Effects of Sleep Deprivation on the Body," Healthline, August 19, 2014, http://www.healthline.com/health/sleep-deprivation/effects-on-body.

9. Paul Kendall, "How Lack of Sleep Affects the Brain," *Daily Mail* (n.d.), http://www.dailymail.co.uk/health/article-47792/How-lack-sleep-affects-brain.html.

10. Nancy A. Melville, "Sleep Deprivation Mimics Psychosis," Medscape, July 21, 2014, http://www.medscape.com/viewarticle/828576.

11. Rebecca M. C. Spencer, "Neurophysiological Basis of Sleep's Function on Memory and Cognition," *ISRN Physiology* 2013, (2013): 1–17. doi:10.1155/2013/619319.

12. "Sleep, Learning, and Memory," Division of Sleep Medicine, Harvard Medical School, December 18, 2007, http://healthysleep.med.harvard.edu/healthy/matters/benefits-of-sleep/learning-memory.

13. Sharon Begley, "Can You Build a Better Brain?" *Newsweek,* January 3, 2011, http://www.newsweek.com/can-you-build-better-brain-66769.

14. James A. Blumenthal, Michael A. Babyak, Kathleen A. Moore, et al. "Effects of Exercise Training on Older Patients with Major Depression," *Archives of Internal Medicine* 159, no. 19 (1999): 2349–56. doi:10.1001/archinte.159.19.2349; and James E. Graves and Barry A. Franklin, *Resistance Training for Health and Rehabilitation* (Champaign, IL: Human Kinetics, 2001).

15. Martin G. Cole and Nandini Dendukuri, "Risk Factors for Depression among Elderly Community Subjects: A Systematic Review and Meta-Analysis," *American Journal of Psychiatry* 160, no. 6 (2003): 1147–56. doi: 10.1176/appi .ajp.160.6.1147.

16. "Eating Processed Meats, but Not Unprocessed Red Meats, May Raise Risk of Heart Disease and Diabetes" (news release), Harvard T. H. Chan School of Public Health, May 17, 2010, https://www.hsph.harvard.edu/news/press-releases /processed-meats-unprocessed-heart-disease-diabetes.

17. National Institutes of Health, AARP, AARP Research, "NIH-AARP Diet and Health Study: Impact of Diet and Lifestyle Factors on Cancer Incidence: Meat and Meat Mutagens," December 2007, http://www.aarp.org/health/medical -research/info-2007/nci_aarp_diabetes.html.

18. Matthew A. Killingsworth and Daniel T. Gilbert, "A Wandering Mind Is an Unhappy Mind," *Science* 330, no. 6006 (2010): 932. doi: 10.1126/science.1192439.

19. https://www.youtube.com/watch?v=Hzgzim5m7oU.

20. Stephen Post and Jill Neimark, *Why Good Things Happen to Good People: How to Live a Longer, Healthier, Happier Life by the Simple Act of Giving* (New York: Broadway Books, 2007).

21. Elizabeth Heubeck, "Boost Your Health with a Dose of Gratitude: If You Want to Get Healthier, Give Thanks," WebMD, 2004, http://www.webmd.com/women/features/gratitute -health-boost#1.

22. Robert Emmons, "Why Gratitude Is Good," Greater Good in Action, November 16, 2010, http://greatergood.berkeley .edu/article/item/why_gratitude_is_good.

23. Robert A. Emmons and Michael E. McCullough, *Highlights from the Research Project on Gratitude and Thankfulness: Dimensions and Perspectives of Gratitude,* University of Miami, fall 2003, http://www.psy.miami.edu/faculty/mmc cullough/Gratitude-Related%20Stuff/highlights_fall_2003 .pdf.

24. Susan Jimison Vitek, "Gratitude Boosts Mental and Physical Health," *Massachusetts General Hospital Mind, Mood, & Memory,* August 2016.

25. Steven Covey, *The 7 Habits of Highly Effective People: Powerful Lessons in Personal Change* (New York: Simon & Schuster, 1989, 2004), 247.

26. Marilyn Hamilton (speech, California Governor and First Lady's Conference on Women, Long Beach, California, September 26, 2006).

27. James Allen, *As a Man Thinketh,* Project Gutenberg eBook, https://www.gutenberg.org/files/4507/4507-h/4507-h.htm.

Bibliography

Allen, James. *As a Man Thinketh*. Melrose, FL: AsAManThinketh .net, 1902, 2001–2012.

Banks, Syd. *The Enlightened Gardener*. Vancouver, BC: Lone Pine, 2005.

Benson, Herbert. *The Relaxation Response*. New York: William Morrow, 1975.

Carlson, Richard. *Don't Sweat the Small Stuff...and It's All Small Stuff*. New York: Hachette Books, 1996.

Carlson, Richard. *You Can Be Happy No Matter What*. Novato, CA: New World Library, 2006.

Carnegie, Dale. *How to Stop Worrying and Start Living*. New York: Pocket Books, 1944, 1984.

Cooper, Kenneth H. *Aerobics*. Lanham, MD: M Evans, 1968.

Covey, Stephen R. *The 7 Habits of Highly Effective People: Powerful Lessons in Personal Change*. New York: Simon & Schuster, 1989, 2004.

Crowley, Chris, and Henry S. Lodge. *Younger Next Year: The Exercise Program*. New York: Workman, 2015.

Csikszentmihalyi, Mihaly. *Flow: The Psychology of Optimal Experience*. New York: Harper Perennial, 1990, 2009.

Goleman, Daniel. *Emotional Intelligence: Why It Can Matter More Than IQ*. New York: Bantam Books, 1995, 2005.

Leonard, Jon N., Jack L. Hofer, and Nathan Pritikin. *Live Longer Now: The First One Hundred Years of Your Life.* New York: Ace Books, 1974.

Loehr, Jim, and Tony Schwartz. *The Power of Full Engagement: Managing Energy, Not Time, Is the Key to High Performance and Personal Renewal.* New York: Free Press Paperbacks, 2003.

Lyubomirsky, Sonja. *The How of Happiness: A New Approach to Getting the Life You Want.* New York: Penguin, 2007.

Norville, Deborah. *Thank You Power: Making the Science of Gratitude Work for You.* Nashville: Thomas Nelson, 2007.

Novak, David. *Taking People with You: The Only Way to Make Big Things Happen.* New York: Portfolio/Penguin, 2012.

Pransky, George S. *The Renaissance of Psychology.* Woodmere, NY: Sulzberger & Graham, 1998.

Schwartz, Tony. *Be Excellent at Anything: The Four Keys to Transforming the Way We Work and Live.* New York: Free Press, 2011.

Selby, John. *Quiet Your Mind: An Easy-to-Use Guide to Ending Chronic Worry and Negative Thoughts and Living a Calmer Life.* Makawao, HI: Inner Ocean, 2004.

Seligman, Martin E. P. *Flourish: A Visionary New Understanding of Happiness and Well-Being.* New York: Free Press, 2011.

Wiseman, Richard. *The Luck Factor: The Four Essential Principles.* New York: Hyperion, 2003.

Acknowledgments

More people than I can mention here have helped keep me up the Mood Elevator, helped me understand the principles underlying it, and provided life lessons in its use.

If I am to start where my understanding first began, I must first thank my mother, whom we all call Nana. She told me over and over again at a very young age that the feelings that are up the Mood Elevator—like love, self-confidence, and wisdom—were God-given gifts that I was born with and that only error in my thinking could keep me from them.

Some of my greatest life lessons over the past 50 years have come by way of raising my five wonderful children: Kevin, Darin, Jason, Kendra, and Logan. They continue to teach me about unconditional love, caring, a purpose beyond myself, being present, and the joy of life through the eyes of a child.

My companion, soul mate, and guide in mastering the concepts underlying the Mood Elevator is my wife, Bernadette. She helps me live them every day and understands them better than I do.

Bernadette and Paul Nakai introduced me to Sydney Banks, the originator of the three principles that formed the foundation of the Mood Elevator, and to George and Linda Pransky of Pransky and Associates, who first taught those principles to Senn Delaney and me.

I owe thanks to Karl Weber, a superb writer and editor, who helped me sharpen and improve the book; and to Neal Mallet at Berrett-Koehler, who convinced me they were the best partner with whom to publish the book.

Index

AARP study, 112

accountability, 35, 54

adaptiveness, 87

adjusting to environment, 46, 87

adversity, 130–133, 155–159

aerobic exercise, 105–108

air travel examples, 94–96, 97–98

Allen, James, 162–163

American Banker, 38

anaerobic exercise, 107–108

anger, feeding/starving, 80–82

anxiety. *See* worry/anxiety

Apple, 64, 65

appreciation. *See* gratitude/appreciation

Archives of Internal Medicine, 107

As a Man Thinketh (Allen), 162–163

assumptions
    about motives of others, 151–153
    about others' behaviors, 149–150
    making positive, 149–150
    of positive intention, 144–148
    wrong, 64–65

AT&T, 52–53

attention. *See* awareness/paying attention

attitudes
    dysfunctional, 54–55
    lighthearted, 95
    mild preference, 91–93
    organizational, 39
    role of thoughts in shaping, 151–152
    transforming, 72–73
    in upper levels of Mood Elevator, 35

authenticity, 35

"A Wandering Mind Is
    an Unhappy Mind"
    (Killingsworth and
    Gilbert), 118
awareness/paying attention
    to feelings in relationships,
    49–50
    to unhealthy state, 48
    to warning signs of
        unhealthy normal,
        54–56
    to your mood/emotions,
    44

Ballmer, Steve, 64
Banks, Sydney, 50
behaviors
    beliefs about others', 90
    challenges to our, 158–159
    dealing inappropriate,
        28–29
    effects on others' thoughts
        of our, 18–19
    healthy/unhealthy, 33
    organizational, 33
    patterns of, 49–50
    role of thoughts in shaping,
        151–152
    in upper levels of Mood
        Elevator, 35
being here now, 116–118, 119

being in the zone (flow
    times), 26
being states, 116
beliefs
    challenges to, 158–159
    deep-seated, 90
    wrong, 64–65
Bell Atlantic, 52–53
Benson, Herbert, 119–120
best self, reconnecting with
    your, 27–28
Bezos, Jeff, 31
blame-game mentality, 53–54,
    85, 141
    avoiding the, 144–148
boiling-frog metaphor, 45–46,
    47
bother. *See* irritation/being
    bothered
braking systems
    curiosity as, 81
    of elevators, 57–58
breathing
    as pattern interrupt, 70
    for quiet mind, 119–120,
        177

Carlson, Richard, 90
CEO Show, 38
challenges, 130–133

Cherokee legend, 77

Chief Executive, 38

children, thought habits of, 27–28

choices, 78–79

circadian cycle, 102

clearing your mind, 25–26

collaboration, 52, 172

collective intelligence, 31

communication
    cautious, 169
    during low-mood states, 167
    of your ideas, 142–143

composure, keeping your, 28–29

confidence, 161–162

conflicts. *See* disagreements/ conflicts

connections, personal to organizational, 35

consciousness
    principles of, 90

consciousness principle, 50

contagious quality of moods, 70–71

Cooper, Kenneth, 105, 110

Cooper Clinic, 106

core beliefs, Senn Delaney's, 33

Cossman, E. Joseph, 102

Covey, Stephen, 144

creativity, 85–86

Csikszentmihalyi, Mihaly, 26

cultural issues
    culture of rivalry, 52–53
    keeping the culture, 20
    merging of cultures, 63–64
    neglecting, 39
    organizational culture, 34, 39, 51–54

culture shaping
    core beliefs and, 33–34
    effects of, 66
    with executive teams, 104
    fostering high-performing, 51–53
    L Brands', 37
    using the Mood Elevator, 38

curiosity
    as brake, 81
    choosing, 65–66
    for disagreements, 142
    living life with more, 58
    responding with, 61

customer surveys, 38–39

daily life, 14–15, 24

dashboard. *See* human dashboard

Dayton Hudson, 53

decision making, 104

deep breathing, 70

defensiveness, 85

Department of Veterans
    Affairs, MyVA Advisory
    Committee, 39

depression
    as mood driver, 6, 15
    nature of, 82–84
    sleep deprivation and, 103
    sources of, 3, 15
    See also mood(s)

despair, 83–84

diet/nutrition, 109–114

"Dimensions and Perspectives
    of Gratitude," 126

disagreements/conflicts
    examples, 49, 58, 93, 141,
        144
    going to curiosity for, 142
    ground rules for managing,
        167–168
    making fresh starts,
        148–150
    managing, 143–144

disaster scenarios, 44, 157

disastrous events, 157–159

diseases/illnesses. *See* physical
    fitness

doing down well analogy,
    166, 169

*Don't Sweat the Small Stuff
    and It's All Small Stuff*
    (Carlson), 90

dysfunctional habits.
    See habits

elevator braking systems,
    57–58

Emmons, Robert A., 126

emotional intelligence, 147

emotions/feelings
    finding support for, 41
    as gift, 41–42
    as guides, 42, 143–144, 176
    habitual emotional states,
        47–48
    impatience-related, 43
    intense, 164
    Mood Elevator concept
        and, 5–6
    negative, 24, 73–75, 78–82
    noticing and responding
        with, 97
    positive, 8–9
    reacting with, 152–153
    research on effects of,
        125–126, 127
    resisting emotional
        impulses, 59–61, 66
    thoughts as triggers of, 176

ups and downs of, 4–5, 41
See also worry/anxiety

employees
importance of culture to, 20
L Brands' surveyed, 37–38
Southwest Airlines, 94–95
See also teams/teamwork

endorphins, 70, 108

energy pumps and drains, 71

Enron, 51–52, 152

environment, unconscious adjustment to, 46

Essential Organizational Values, 35, 36–39

ethics, 52, 92

events, how you think about, 16

exercise, 70, 105–109, 126–127

eyewitness testimony, 137–138

faith
forms of, 160
power of, 159–163
through adversity, 177
true meaning of, 163–164

familiarity blindness, 51

family relationships, 129, 172

faulty memories, 138

faulty thinking, 96–98

fish bobber example, 28

fitness. *See* physical fitness

flexibility, 87

Flourish (Seligman), 128

flow times (being in the zone), 26

food choices, 109–114

forgiving/forgiveness, 81, 150–153

Fortune magazine, 32, 37, 51

fraud, corporate, 52

fresh starts, 148–150

Fricchione, Gregory L., 127

frog metaphor, 45–46, 47

Gallup polls, 32

Gilbert, Daniel, 118

gratitude/appreciation, 8–9, 86
accessing, 128–129
benefits of, 124–127
choosing the gratitude perspective, 122–124
effect on others of, 147–148
in the face of adversity, 130–133

gratitude/appreciation
(continued)
maintaining perspective
of, 177
"Power of Words" video,
121–122
sharing appreciation, 129
unconditional, 133–135

habits
being in the zone, 26
blame game, 53–54
depression, 82–83
life practices, 99–100
as obstructions to health,
27–28
unhealthy normal, 51
worry, 79, 85
habitual emotional states,
47–48
Hamilton, Marilyn, 155–157
happiness, 118, 126–127
Harvard School of Public
Health data, 112
health issues
healthy behaviors, 33
innate health, 175,
176–178
potential for health, 27
problems of, 131–132
See also physical fitness

Heidrick & Struggles, 20
higher mood states, 172–173
higher purpose, finding your,
73–75
higher-quality thinking,
25–26, 116, 132.
See also upper floors of
Mood Elevator
Hofer, Jack L., 110
hope/hopefulness, 86,
160–161, 163–164
hostility, 49
The How of Happiness
(Lyubomirsky), 126–127
human condition, 5
human dashboard, 42–45
humility, 141–142
humor/laughter, 93–96

ideas, original, 30–32
illnesses/diseases. *See* physical
fitness
illusionist example, 29
imagination, 18–19, 165–166
impatience, 43, 84
impulses, emotional, 59–61
injustice, 141
innate health, 175, 176–178

inner dialogue, making a movie in your head, 18–21

innocence, assuming, 150–153

innovative thinking, 65, 85–86

insecurity, 85

insights, new, 31

integrity, 35, 52

intelligence, collective, 31

intensity, 47, 48

Internet, 31, 102

irritation/being bothered, 6, 7, 9, 10, 54
  avoiding, 100
  boiling-frog metaphor, 45–46, 47
  with judgmentalism, 141, 171
  justifying, 149
  letting go of, 150–151
  managing, 81, 97–98, 100, 122, 168, 171–172
  prolonged, 91
  reacting with, 61, 64, 84–85, 89–90, 144, 145–147
  reactions to feeling, 85, 89–90
  relationships and, 172–173
  See also rigidity

J.D. Power award, 32

JL Hudson, 53–54

John Templeton Foundation, 126

journal writing, 126, 128

judgmentalism, 61–65, 66, 85, 141, 149–150

karma, 172

Killingsworth, Matthew, 118

Kramer, Arthur F., 105

laughter/humor, 93–96

L Brands, 36–37

learning from experiences, 58–59

Leonard, Jon N., 110

life challenges, 130–133

lifestyle choices, 113

lighter thinking, 96–98

little things in life, 91–93

Live Longer Now (Leonard, Hofer, and Pritikin), 110

losing your cool, 28–29

love, unconditional, 133

lower floors of the Mood Elevator, 6, 9, 11, 84–85
  impatience, 43

lower floors of the Mood
  Elevator *(continued)*
  line between upper floors
    and, 58
  nature of thoughts on, 115
  worry, 44
lower-level thinking, 25, 78,
  97, 116
low-mood states, 75–76,
  171–173, 177
  doing down well analogy,
    166, 169
  imagination and, 165–166
  reliability of thinking in,
    166–168
luck factor, 173–174
The Luck Factor (Wiseman),
  173
Lyubomirsky, Sonja, 126–127

mantras, 119
meaning of faith, 163–164
memories, 30–31, 138
mental eddies, 72
mental fitness
  recovery cycle, 102–105
  stretch-and-recover cycle
    for, 101–102
  See also physical fitness
mental movies, 18–21

mental traction, maintaining
  your, 28–29
Microsoft, 64
mild preferences, 91–93, 97
mind/body connection, 70
mind principle, 50
mind, principles of, 90
mind-sets, 27–28, 35,
  128–129
mistakes, 76, 145–146
mood drivers
  deep breathing, 70
  exercise, 70
  organizational values,
    33–39
  self-talk, 72
  sleep, 69
  sources of, 13–17
  thoughts as, 19–21, 23–24
Mood Elevator concept
  braking system in, 58–59
  as feelings barometer, 42
  floors of the, 5–6, 7
  pocket card for, 45
  pointers for riding the
    Mood Elevator, 175–178
  reflecting on role of, 8
  relationship among floors
    of, 11–12
  riding the, 4–5

in *Taking People with You* (Novak), 38

mood(s)
awareness of your, 44
changing your, 32
choosing which to feed, 84–87
contagiousness of, 70–71
feeling down (*See* low-mood states)
habitual, 47
influence on others of, 71–72
of others, 29–30
thinking as creator of, 41
See also depression

motivation(s), drivers of, 81

movies in your mind, 18–21, 68

mustard seed analogy, 161–162

National Institutes of Health, 112

natural state, 27–28, 178

negative thoughts/feelings, 24, 73–75, 78–82. *See also* pattern interrupts

non–rapid eye movement (NREM) sleep, 103

normal. *See* unhealthy-normal states

Norville, Deborah, 128

Novak, David, 38

NREM (non–rapid eye movement) sleep, 103

nutrition/diet, 109–114

Obama, Barack, 39

off time, 117

optimism, 83, 86, 164

organizational culture, 34, 39, 51–54

organizational payoffs of going up the Mood Elevator, 32–34

organizational values, 33–39

original ideas, 30–32

outcomes, seeking the right, 157–159

overriding emotions, 122–123

patience, 86–87

pattern interrupts
example of, 67–69
failures of, 75–76
focusing on higher purpose, 73–75
• using, 177

pattern interrupts *(continued)*
  varieties of, 69–73
  with worry, 79

patterns, recognizing
    unhealthy, 55

payoffs. *See* organizational
    payoffs of going up
    the Mood Elevator;
    personal payoffs
    of going up the
    Mood Elevator

perception(s)
  appreciating others', 142
  differing, 138–139, 140
  See also perspective(s)

performance, sleep
    deprivation and,
    102–103

personal payoffs of going up
    the Mood Elevator
  access to original ideas,
    30–32
  maintaining your mental
    traction, 28–29
  reconnecting with your
    best self, 27–28
  for understanding power
    of thought, 24–26

perspective(s)
  acceptance of differing, 141
  on adverse events, 159

appreciating others',
    142–144
  changes in, 134–135
  developing a sense of, 93
  gratitude, 122–124
  how to state your, 143
  putting problems into,
    95–96
  regaining, 30
  separate realities, 139–142
  on your mood, 76

petitionary prayer, 157

physical fitness, 44
  exercise, 70, 105–109
  food choices, 109–114
  getting enough sleep,
    102–105
  importance of, 100, 177
  stretch-and-recover cycle,
    101–102
  through gratitude, 125

pleasure, 8–9

point of view. *See*
    perspective(s)

positive emotions, 8–9

positive intentions, 144–148

positive thoughts
  attention to, 163–164
  living in mild preference
    for, 92–93

Post, Stephen, 125

power of thought
  effect on emotions, 19–21
  payoffs from
    understanding, 24–26
  reducing the, 21

Pransky, George, 49–50

Pransky, Linda, 49

prayer, petitionary, 157

principles of mind, thought,
    consciousness, 50, 90,
    92

Pritikin, Nathan, 110–112

Pritikin diet, 111–112

problems/problem solving
  going up the Mood
    Elevator for, 25–26
  during REM sleep, 104
  sources of solutions, 32

purpose, finding your higher,
    73–75

Quickie wheelchairs, 156–157

quiet mind
  for accessing gratitude,
    128–129
  being here now, 116–118
  breathing technique for,
    119–120

Quiet Your Mind (Selby), 120

rapid eye movement (REM)
    sleep, 103–104

reactions
  assumptions as drivers of,
    149–150
  to confusing events, 60–61
  emotion-based, 152–153
  irritation/being bothered,
    61, 64, 84–85, 89–90,
    144, 145–147
  as mood drivers, 15
  pausing before, 97

reading interpretation
    example, 59–61

reality(ies), living in separate,
    139–142

reconnecting with your best
    self, 27–28

recovery periods, 101–102,
    116

relationships
  attention to your feelings
    in, 49
  changes in thinking about
    different, 16–17
  dysfunctional, 172
  family, 129, 172
  fostering good, 173–174
  ground rules for, 167–168
  irritation/bother within,
    90–91

relationships *(continued)*
  living in mild preference
    for, 93
  making friends, not
    enemies, 172
  mutually supportive, 35
  positive and negative,
    71–72
  skills for, 173–174
  ties between Mood
    Elevator and, 172–173
  unhealthy normal and,
    49–50
  using the Mood Elevator
    for building, 171–173
The Relaxation Response
  (Benson), 119–120
REM (rapid eye movement)
  sleep, 103–104
resistance training, 107–108
riding the Mood Elevator,
  4–6, 175–178
right outcomes, praying for,
  157
right thinking, 163
right/wrong dynamic, 53,
  62–63
rigidity, 90, 93–96, 98
risk taking, 35
rivalry, culture of, 52–53
Robles, Josue "Joe," Jr., 38–39

rumors, anxiety caused by,
  1–4
rushing to judgment, 62

seeing is believing, 137–138
Selby, John, 120
self-actualization, 123
self-awareness, 44
self-care, 100
self-centered mind-set, 27
self-confidence, 161–162
self-destructive way of life, 48
self-interest, 52
self-reflection, flow times
  during, 26
self-reinforcement, 75
self-talk, 72
Seligman, Martin, 128
Senn Delaney, 5, 18, 20, 32,
  46, 51–54, 131, 148,
  152, 159, 169. *See also*
  culture shaping
separate realities, 139–142,
  177
set point
  for happiness, 126–127
  on the Mood Elevator,
    99–100, 108–109
sleep, 69, 102–105, 109

small stuff, 90, 91–93, 130

Smith, Ray, 52–53

snap judgments, 64

solutions. *See* problems/
　　problem solving

Southwest Airlines example,
　　94–96

Spencer, Rebecca, 103–104

spirit, positive, 35

standards, 62, 90, 92, 161

state of grace, 134

states of health, 48

states of mind
　　being state, 116–117
　　grace, 134
　　habitual emotional states,
　　　47–48
　　higher mood states,
　　　172–173
　　natural state, 27–28, 178
　　See also mood(s);
　　　unhealthy-normal states

strength training, 107–108

stress
　　effects of, 7, 8, 10, 78, 147,
　　　167
　　managing, 32, 66, 68, 72,
　　　94–95, 103, 108, 117,
　　　164
　　recovery from, 116

responses to, 28

sources of, 100, 132

stretch-and-recover cycle,
　　101–102

stretching, 107–108

subjectivity, 139–140

success
　　enjoyment of life for, 24
　　higher levels of Mood
　　　Elevator and, 10–11
　　in life and organizations,
　　　39

teams/teamwork
　　collaboration, 52, 172
　　culture shaping with, 104
　　team members, 148–150

Thank You Power (Norville),
　　128

thought principle, 50

thoughts/thinking
　　as barrier to success,
　　　162–163
　　being in the zone, 26
　　categories of our, 30
　　changes in, 16, 84
　　choosing what to focus on,
　　　124
　　clearing your mind, 25–26
　　faith as driver of, 161–162
　　faulty thinking, 96–98

thoughts/thinking
(*continued*)
feeding your thoughts, 78, 177
habits of, 27–28, 176
higher-quality, 24
influence on emotions of, 23
innovative, 65
listening to your, 41
in low-mood states, 166–168
memory-based, 31
negative, 24, 73–75, 78–82
power of, 19–20
principles of, 90
quality of our, 25
reliability of your, 42
role in shaping attitudes and behaviors of, 151–152
switching your train of thought, 67–69
thinking more lightly, 96–98
understanding power of, 24–26
See also pattern interrupts
time off, 117
traction example, 29
train of thought, 67

transparency, 35
tug-of-war example, 29

unconditional gratitude, 133–135
unconscious habits, 53
unconsciousness, unhealthy-normal state and, 45–49
understanding others, 86–87, 144. *See also* perspective(s)
unhappiness, habitual, 47
unhealthy behaviors, 33, 176
unhealthy-normal states
identifying your, 54–55
in organizations, 51–54
phenomenon of, 45–49
in relationships, 49–50
in thought patterns, 176
unconsciousness, 45–49
warning signs, 54–56
upper floors of Mood Elevator, 5–6, 8–9, 11
benefits of, 99
examples of living on, 144–148
line between lower floors and, 58
mental fitness and, 101–102

USAA, 38–39

USA Today, 64

use it or lose it principle, 105–108

us-versus-them mentality, 172

values, organizational, 33–39

views, differing, 139–142

violence, 141

wandering mind, 118, 120. *See also* quiet mind

"A Wandering Mind Is an Unhappy Mind" (Killingsworth and Gilbert), 117

Warren Distribution Center, 53–54

water supply example, 68–69

Wexner, Les, 37–38

win-lose and win-win dynamics, 27, 33, 35, 53, 173

Wiseman, Richard, 173

wolf legend, 77

work time, 117

worry/anxiety
example (John's story), 1–4, 14, 15–16, 41
feeding/starving, 78–79, 85
as mood driver, 15
as motivator, 79
recognizing onset of, 72
recovery from, 116
sources of, 2
stopping the worry cycle, 44
See also emotions/feelings

yoga, 108

YUM! Brands, 38

About the Author

Larry Senn, PhD, is a father, grandfather, husband, author, lecturer, CEO coach, and fitness enthusiast. He is the founder and chair of Senn Delaney, a Heidrick & Struggles company, and the oldest, most experienced, and most successful organizational culture–shaping firm in the world.

Dr. Senn has been referred to in business journals as "the father of corporate culture." His early experience in running a traditional consulting firm led him to conclude that too many organizations were like dysfunctional families. He saw that the habits of well-intentioned people reduced both the spirit and the performance of even the best organizations. It made them less fulfilling places to work, and it made getting results harder than need be.

That realization inspired the first research ever conducted on the concept of corporate culture as a part of Larry's doctoral dissertation, published in 1970. It led to an early personal vision of finding a way to enhance the lives of people, the effectiveness of teams, and the spirit and performance of organizations. That vision became Senn Delaney.

211

Because organizational transformation requires personal transformation, concepts and processes were developed that touched individuals. Participants found that the concepts of leadership effectiveness were also principles of life effectiveness.

The Mood Elevator was one of those concepts. It is the one that has been most universally embraced, retained, and used by people in their lives at work and at home. To date, nearly a million people in 40 countries around the world have been exposed to the Mood Elevator. They have been part of the Senn Delaney process in organizations of all kinds, from business corporations, to hospitals, to schools and universities, to governments at all levels.

This is Senn Delaney's vision today: *To positively impact the world by inspiring leaders to create thriving cultures that enhance the spirit and performance of organizations.*

The aim of this book is to better support all of the people who have been exposed to Senn Delaney concepts and to take the Mood Elevator to individuals in the world beyond Senn Delaney's client organizations.

Larry lives in Sunset Beach, California, with his wife, Bernadette, and their teenage son, Logan. They have a daughter, Kendra; three older sons, Kevin, Darin, and Jason; and five grandchildren.

Larry and Bernadette have a deep commitment to fitness and well-being. Bernadette is a competitive runner, and Larry runs, bikes, swims, and competes in a half dozen triathlons a year.

For more information about Senn Delaney, visit www.senndelaney.com. For bulk book orders, to inquire about conference presentations, or to contact Larry Senn about how the Mood Elevator can impact your organization's culture, e-mail larry@themoodelevator.com or visit www.themoodelevator.com.

Berrett–Koehler
Publishers

Berrett-Koehler is an independent publisher dedicated to an ambitious mission: *Connecting people and ideas to create a world that works for all.*

We believe that the solutions to the world's problems will come from all of us, working at all levels: in our organizations, in our society, and in our own lives. Our BK Business books help people make their organizations more humane, democratic, diverse, and effective (we don't think there's any contradiction there). Our BK Currents books offer pathways to creating a more just, equitable, and sustainable society. Our BK Life books help people create positive change in their lives and align their personal practices with their aspirations for a better world.

All of our books are designed to bring people seeking positive change together around the ideas that empower them to see and shape the world in a new way.

And we strive to practice what we preach. At the core of our approach is Stewardship, a deep sense of responsibility to administer the company for the benefit of all of our stakeholder groups including authors, customers, employees, investors, service providers, and the communities and environment around us. Everything we do is built around this and our other key values of quality, partnership, inclusion, and sustainability.

This is why we are both a B-Corporation and a California Benefit Corporation—a certification and a for-profit legal status that require us to adhere to the highest standards for corporate, social, and environmental performance.

We are grateful to our readers, authors, and other friends of the company who consider themselves to be part of the BK Community. We hope that you, too, will join us in our mission.

A BK Life Book

BK Life books help people clarify and align their values, aspirations, and actions. Whether you want to manage your time more effectively or uncover your true purpose, these books are designed to instigate infectious positive change that starts with you. Make your mark!

To find out more, visit **www.bkconnection.com**.

Berrett–Koehler
Publishers

Connecting people and ideas
to create a world that works for all

Dear Reader,

Thank you for picking up this book and joining our worldwide community of Berrett-Koehler readers. We share ideas that bring positive change into people's lives, organizations, and society.

To welcome you, we'd like to offer you a free e-book. You can pick from among twelve of our bestselling books by entering the promotional code **BKP92E** here: http://www.bkconnection.com/welcome.

When you claim your free e-book, we'll also send you a copy of our e-newsletter, the *BK Communiqué*. Although you're free to unsubscribe, there are many benefits to sticking around. In every issue of our newsletter you'll find

- A free e-book
- Tips from famous authors
- Discounts on spotlight titles
- Hilarious insider publishing news
- A chance to win a prize for answering a riddle

Best of all, our readers tell us, "Your newsletter is the only one I actually read." So claim your gift today, and please stay in touch!

Sincerely,

Charlotte Ashlock
Steward of the BK Website

Questions? Comments? Contact me at bkcommunity@bkpub.com.